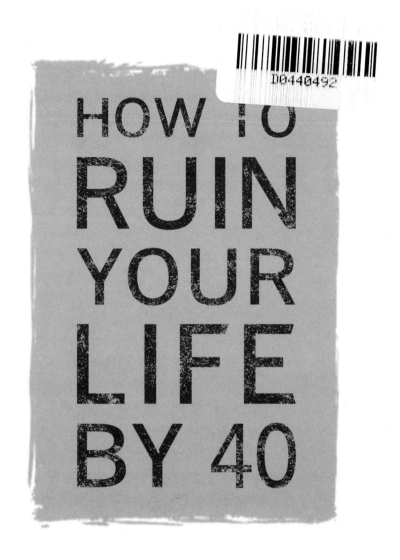

HOW TO RUIN YOUR LIFE BY 40

STEVE FARRAR

MOODY PUBLISHERS
Chicago

Scripture quotations, unless otherwise indicated, are taken from the *New American
Standard Bible*, Copyright © 1960, 1962, 1963, 1968, 1971, 1972, 1973, 1975, 1977, 1995 by
The Lockman Foundation. Used by permission.

Scripture quotations marked NKJV are taken from the *New King James Version*, Copyright
© 1982 by Thomas Nelson, Inc. Used by permission. All rights reserved.

All italics added to Scripture quotations are the author's emphasis.

Cover Design: Wes Youssi | www.thedesignworksgroup.com
Image Credit: Photodisc (bomb image)
Photography Credit: Steve Gardner | www.shootpw.com
Editor: Ali Diaz

Library of Congress Cataloging-in-Publication Data

Farrar, Steve.
  How to ruin your life by 40 / Steve Farrar.
     p. cm.
  Includes bibliographical references.
  ISBN-13: 978-0-8024-3322-0
  1. Success—Religious aspects—Christianity. 2. Young adults—Religious life. 3. Young
adults—Conduct of life. I. Title. II. Title: How to ruin your life by forty.

BV4598.3.F37 2006
248.8'4—dc22

                                                              2006019839

ISBN: 0-8024-3322-7
ISBN 13: 978-0-8024-3322-0

We hope you enjoy this book from Moody Publishers. Our goal is to provide
high-quality, thought-provoking books and products that connect truth to your real
needs and challenges. For more information on other books and products written and
produced from a biblical perspective, go to www.moodypublishers.com or write to:

Moody Publishers
820 N. LaSalle Boulevard
Chicago, IL 60610

1 3 5 7 9 10 8 6 4 2

Printed in the United States of America

"*The first years of man must make provision for the last. He that never thinks can never be wise. Perpetual levity must end in ignorance; and intemperance, though it may fire the spirits for an hour, will make life short or miserable. Let us consider that youth is of no long duration, and that in maturer age, when the enchantments of fancy shall cease, and phantoms of delight dance no more about us, we shall have no comforts but the esteem of wise men and the means of doing good. Let us, therefore, stop, while to stop is in our power: let us live as men who are sometime to grow old.*"

—from *Rasselas*, by Samuel Johnson

CONTENTS

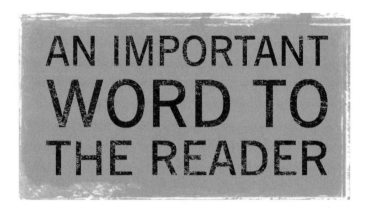

AN IMPORTANT WORD TO THE READER

This book did not begin as a book. It began as a twenty-minute graduation address for high school students at Coram Deo Academy in Flower Mound, Texas. It was graduation day for my son Josh and his fellow classmates. My address was titled "How To Ruin Your Life By 40."

Approximately eighteen months later, I was invited to speak at Biola University in La Mirada, California, for their annual Torrey Conference. Josh and his older brother, John, were both students at Biola. As we were talking one day about the upcoming conference, they both said I ought to expand my "How To Ruin Your Life By 40" talk. So I did.

About six months later, Mark Tobey at Moody Publishers said, "Steve, you ought to take your talks on how to ruin your life by 40 that you did at Biola and turn them into a book." So here it is.

Now this is where things can get really boring. This is the point where authors begin to thank everyone who helped them put the book together. It's a good thing to be thankful for gifted people. But if you're not careful, you can turn your thanks into a literary version of a ten-minute Oscar acceptance speech.

So this is going to be real short but real important.

There are a lot of people I could thank, including my wife, Mary, who edits everything I write and makes suggestions that sometimes drive me nuts the first time she runs them by me. But her keen eye is almost always on target. It's great to have a wife who is on your team. And we've been a team for almost thirty years now.

My daughter, Rachel, read this book in its earliest stages and made some very astute observations that probed my thinking. She's been doing that since she was three. John read it as well and gave me some of his wise discernment in several critical spots. Kathryn Harris read the opening chapters at our kitchen counter and gave me some excellent feedback. I told her I would thank her in the book. She didn't think I was serious.

But the guy who I really need to thank is Josh. In many ways, he was my coauthor on this book. He helped me take my four core talks and rework them and expand them from beginning to end. I've quoted Josh at some points in the book. But those quotes represent a very small amount of his contribution. On this book he was my cothinker and copilot. This book simply wouldn't have happened without Josh Farrar.

It's important to me that you know that.

Steve Farrar

If you want to ruin your life by forty, then ignore the law of cause and effect.

CHAPTER 1

CAUSE AND EFFECT

At eighteen years of age, Jane Lucretia D'Esterre was talented and beautiful. As she stood on the bank of a beautiful, deep lake in Scotland, she pondered plunging into the depths and taking her life. She had lost all hope. The year was 1815, and her husband, John, had just been killed in a duel. He left her penniless, in a new country, completely by herself, with two babies to care for. Her family was in France, and she was without any kind of support: emotional, spiritual, or financial.

As she gazed into the depths of the lake and pondered the pain and brokenness of her life, she looked up and saw a young man on the other side of the lake plowing furrows on the hillside. He was completely focused on his work. He was not aware of her gaze as he guided the plow behind the horse with a single-minded purpose.

In her moment of despair, she was so impressed with the young plowman's focus and concentration on doing his work well, that his example and concentration pulled her out of her despair. Suddenly, she was infused with hope. She was also given a timely dose of wisdom. She knew what she was supposed to do. She needed to move straight ahead as the young plowman was doing. She, too, had a meaningful task to fulfill. Her children needed her. They had lost one parent already—they didn't need to experience the loss of another.

When she looked at the young man's example, she was given wisdom. Or to put it another way, she was given a wise heart. And when her heart became wise, it then became brave to do the right and hard thing.

A few weeks after this experience at the lake, Jane came to faith in Christ. A few years later she married Captain John Grattan Guinness, who was the youngest son of the famous brewer, Arthur Guinness.

Os Guinness tells this story in his excellent book *The Call*. Os is a gifted Christian author who has influenced many toward the kingdom of God. Jane D'Esterre was Os Guinness's great-great-grandmother. Os comments on the significance of the events that took place in Jane's life when she was just eighteen:

> If it had not been for the duel, our side of the family would not have come into being. If it had not been for the plowman, the tragedy of the dueling husband would have been followed by the tragedy of the duelist's widow. . . .
>
> My great-great-grandmother was unusual for several reasons—including the fact that she conscientiously prayed for her descendants down through a dozen generations. Ours is a heritage of faith, for which I, for one, am extremely grateful.[1]

When eighteen-year-old Jane was gazing into the deep, dark depths of the lake and pondering death, she couldn't see five generations ahead and see Os Guinness or any of her other descendants. All she could see was that her life was finished. But it wasn't finished. By looking at a purposeful young man plowing on a hill, she realized there was hope. She could take the path of the lake or she could take the life of moving ahead, in spite of her mind-numbing emotional pain.

She had no idea that Christ would call her to forgiveness and purpose in just a matter of weeks. She couldn't imagine that she would have another husband who would love her and her children. All she knew at that moment was that she could choose death or life.

She had a choice to make, and that choice would carry consequences.

That concept is known as cause and effect.

With the wrong choice she could have ruined her life and her future. With the wrong choice she would ruin the childhood of her young children.

But she made the right choice as an eighteen-year-old. And her family is still grateful today that she did, nearly two hundred years later.

The choices you are making in your life are just as significant.

THE FIRST TWENTY YEARS

In the first twenty years of your life, your parents make the major decisions for you.

From twenty on out, you will be making the decisions. The quality of your decisions will determine what your life will look like at forty. So from here on, the ball is in your court.

You are no longer a kid. You are an adult. And it will be the choices that you make over the next few years that will make you or break you by forty.

And forty will be here before you know it. If you don't believe that, just ask someone who's there.

So when do you actually become an adult?

That's kind of hard to nail down because it happens in phases. As far as the law is concerned, eighteen is a very real marker of adulthood. But the big one is twenty-one. At the age of twenty-one, you have officially entered into the world of adulthood. And you are a full-fledged member, whether you feel like it or not.

My three kids are no longer kids. They have all passed their twenty-first birthdays and are officially adults.

One night at dinner, Josh, who is twenty-two and a senior in college, was giving me some feedback on what he had read. We were talking about the fact that it is a huge transition to go from the teenage years into early adulthood. As I was listening to his feedback, I held up my hand and said, "Wait a minute, this is pretty good stuff. Let me get a pen and write it down."

"You don't need to write it down, Dad. I already did."

"When did you do that, last night?"

"No, I wrote it down about a year ago. I've been giving a lot of thought to this."

So here's what Josh wrote. I asked him to update it for this chapter. See if it doesn't resonate with you and your personal walk into adulthood:

THE DAY OF ALL DAYS

In American culture, it is the first rite of passage into adulthood.

It is the one day every youth looks forward to with more anticipation, more excitement, and more sleeplessness than any other day in life: the day of the driver's license. For a sixteen-year-old, the driver's license is the ticket to a gratifying new world of freedom. By sixteen, the enjoyment of toys without horsepower and rides to the mall from Mom are entirely dissolved, and life has nearly lost its ability to entertain. But to sit in the driver's seat, to hear the car door slam shut, to be left entirely alone, and to feel the surge of power with a push of the pedal—this is the pinnacle of maturity's benefits. The excitement that a new driver feels is an incredible rush, one that he or she can never imagine losing.

But, as we all know, the loss of the thrill of driving is an inevitable occurrence. The roads, once the remedy to all that was boring, eventually become merely roads and nothing more. Then a very strange thing begins to occur. While driving, you are suddenly jolted out of a state of complete distraction to realize you have not focused on the road in what seems to be several minutes. These moments are personal mysteries, attesting to the power of the wandering mind and, I should add, the grace of God. One day you're driving wide-eyed, hugging every turn with intent, and engaging every on-ramp with alertness. The next, you're nearly running into the median, looking up to realize that time has flown by and you were lost in a thought.

Every *action* must have a REACTION.

Life is like driving on a long road trip. You are moving down the highway of life at a very fast clip.

One day you will look up, perhaps after being detained by a very long thought, and realize that you are forty. Life in the twenties is characterized by a continual introduction of new places, new people, and new experiences. Every day is met with a higher level of intent and alertness. But as days pass by like the white lines on the highway, the speed of life increases with every year. Forty will be here before you know it.

But the coming of age and growing old is not what this book is concerned with. There is nothing wrong with wrinkles, and there is nothing shameful about frailty; age is not the enemy. This book is concerned with the coming of consequences—whether good or bad. Deeply ingrained into the fabric of all creation is a law that every action must have a reaction. There are no exceptions to the rule. Every choice in life—every thought, word, and action—brings a return of circumstances with it. The age of forty can only be reached by traveling the road through twenty, twenty-five, and thirty. And the choices in life during those quickly passing years will entirely determine the person you will be at forty.

This is a scary thought, and it should be.

This is also a thought that may seem too obvious and simple to even bring up. Doesn't everyone grasp this concept of cause and effect? Apparently not.

There is not a single person who would answer yes, if asked the question, *Do you want your life to be miserable when you are older?* Yet the majority of young people engage in decisions every day that are leading to that very end. This is evidence of a great disconnect in modern thinking. There is a denial of the law of cause and effect. Many lies have penetrated the mind of this generation, but none greater than this.

Every young man or woman has an image in their head of who they will be in several years, but that image is hardly ever the natural outcome of the life they are living. The truth is that most young people are comforted with a future perception of themselves that is based on the solid evidence of nothing.

This book is intended to realign the disconnect and to awaken a hope for the future that is based upon truth.

MY TWO CENTS

I couldn't agree with Josh more.

Mark it down.

Causes have effects.

Actions have reactions.

Choices have consequences.

That will be the story of your life.

The decision that Jane made as she stood by the lake had consequences. Those consequences have rippled through her descendants for two hundred years. Have you thought about the fact that the decisions you make in the next few years have consequences not only for you but also for your descendants two hundred years from now?

This book is an invitation to think deeply about your life and the critical decisions you will make over the next decade of your life. Wisdom will be the deciding factor. George Moore was right: "The difficulty in life is the choice." When it comes to your personal decisions, you can seek wisdom or ignore it. It's up to you. But your decisions will affect not only you, but also others, some who have yet to be born.

This is no small matter you are facing.

You need the very wisdom of God.

Forty will be here before you know it.

So teach us to number our days,
That we may gain a heart of wisdom. (Psalm 90:12 NKJV)

He gave wisdom to Jane Lucretia D'Esterre to know that her choice would have a consequence.

He is more than willing to give you the same wisdom. And you will need it more than once on the way to forty.

If you want to ruin
your life by forty,
get off to a bad start.

CHAPTER 2

STARTING STRONG, FINISHING STRONG

The Christian life is a race.

When you are in your seventies and eighties, you spend a lot of time thinking about how you're going to finish the race (2 Timothy 4:7).

But in your twenties, you should be thinking about how you're going to start the race.

In any race, the goal is to finish strong. But wouldn't it be great to actually *start* strong? That's where you are right now. You are deciding what kind of start you are going to have.

A lot of people are way beyond the starting line. When you're forty, you're roughly halfway through the race of life.

But you're not forty. So the kind of start you make is still within your control.

The way you begin in life is the *cause* that eventually leads to the effect, or *consequence.* The decade of the twenties determines how you start. The decade of your thirties will be spent living with the *consequences* of those decisions. And how you respond to those consequences, both good and bad, will determine what your life will be like at forty and beyond.

The goal is to start strong. If you start strong and continue in His word (John 8:31–32), then by the grace of God, you will finish strong.

YOUR PAST IS YOUR PAST

Some of you are thinking, *I've already messed up my life.* If that is true, let me encourage you. You are still young. There is great hope for your life. Maybe you are like the prodigal who rebelled in his youth and then came to his senses. Maybe you got involved sexually and now deeply regret it. Maybe you are just beginning to think—really think—about life and choices and their consequences. Don't let regrets hold you back. You are not your past. If you know Christ, you are a redeemed person, set aside for good works.

Have you watched the sprints at the Summer Olympics? I always try to make sure I watch the one-hundred-meter race. The winner is the fastest man in the world. It is not unusual in the one-hundred-meter to have two or three starts. The reason is that all of the sprinters are in the blocks and they are trying to anticipate the starter's gun. If they get just a nanosecond of a head start, it will give them an advantage. So they all line up, and the gun goes off, but someone is called for a false start. So what happens then? They all line up in the blocks and give it another try.

If you've had a false start, God is willing to give you another start. Have you had several false starts? He's still willing to give you another start.

That's what He did with Moses, Peter, and Paul. They all had false starts. But God gave them another opportunity to start over.

Each of them was given another start once they were brought face-to-face with God and His call upon their lives. As a young man, Moses killed an official and had to flee for his life. What if Moses had let his huge mistake as a headstrong young man hold him back from following the call of God? What if Peter's denials of Christ to a young girl had paralyzed his ability to preach and lead the early church? Paul, the murderer of Christians, put it this way in Philippians 3:13–14: "Forgetting what lies behind and reaching forward to what lies ahead, I press on toward the goal for the prize of the upward call of God in Christ Jesus." If Paul could get past his past, so can you. All three turned from their past, accepted God's amazing grace, and set their faces on a path of obedience. And God used them greatly.

The teens are tumultuous years. I don't think I've ever met a Christian man or woman who didn't regret something they did in their formative years. I did some pretty stupid things myself. Many of the lessons in this book I had to learn the hard way. I learned those lessons as I hurt myself and other people. It happens to all of us. But has it occurred to you that God, in His grace, desires to take your past rebellion and sinful choices and turn them to your advantage?

> When God looks around to **use** somebody, He has no one to choose from except **FAILURES.**

Later in this book, we have written a chapter that will go deeper into this subject. But for now, don't let your past—or even your present—keep you from a healthy and hopeful future. Every once in a while someone will tell me that they would like to be used by God, but they know that will never happen. When I ask them why God couldn't use them, they usually tell me about some great failure in their life.

My response to them is that all of us have failed; we just fail in different ways. When God looks around to use somebody, He has no one to choose from except failures. We've all failed, but that doesn't mean that God won't use us. He will actually use that failure to qualify you for the work that He has for you to do.

In the eighteenth century, John Newton was captain of a slave ship when he came to Christ. He was so overwhelmed with the depth of God's love and goodness that he took his pen and wrote a descriptive hymn of God's grace. He could never have known that three hundred years later people would still be singing that great hymn "Amazing Grace." Newton once wrote:

> We serve a gracious Master who knows how to overrule even our mistakes to His glory and our own advantage.

All of his life, John Newton could hear the voices of the slaves that were chained in his ship. He would sometimes hear their cries in the middle of the night as he was dreaming. He would wake up with tremendous regret—and then marvel that he had been forgiven. Not only had he been forgiven, but he was being used by God in spite of his old life. If you are living with regrets over a bad start, accept His grace and goodness, and step back up to the starting line. It's time to get back in the race that counts.

ONE OUT OF TEN

A number of years ago, I wrote a book titled *Finishing Strong.* And in that book I told the story of John Bisagno. John is now retired, but he pastored in Houston for many years.

When Bisagno was twenty-one, he was very excited. He was getting ready to graduate from college and marry the love of his life. He had also decided to go into full-time ministry. He was very optimistic about his future. One night, he was having dinner at his fiancée's home. After dinner, he went outside on the porch with his future father-in-law, Dr. Paul Beck. Dr. Beck had been in ministry since he was John's age. You could say he'd seen a lot of water go under the bridge. As they were talking about John's future plans and dreams, Dr. Beck gave him some advice, "As you go into ministry, John, make sure you stay close to Christ every day."

Young John replied, "Yes, sir. I know that's important."

His future father-in-law continued:

You're just getting started in this race. And it's a very long race. You won't hit the finish line until you're in your seventies or eighties. The finish line is a long way off, John. But the goal of this race is to finish strong. And that's the last thing that Satan wants you to do. That's why you have to keep your heart close to Christ every day. It's been my experience that for every ten men who start strong with Christ in their twenties, only one out of those ten will finish strong.

That shocked John Bisagno. The staggering statistic left him in disbelief.

"That can't be. Just one out of ten?"

"Unfortunately, that has been my experience. Some men are taken out by the love of money, others are taken out by theological liberalism, and many more are taken out by sexual immorality. Satan knows how to lay a trap and set an ambush. He knows every man's weaknesses. That's why it's been my experience that only one out of ten will finish strong."

John Bisagno was blown away by the remarks of the older man. He was so stunned that he went home and started thinking about his friends. They were all in their early twenties and all had bright futures.

They were fully committed followers of Christ.

He was graduating from a Bible college, and many of his buddies, like him, were going to be pastors, missionaries, youth leaders, and worship ministers. He couldn't believe that only one out of ten would finish strong. The very idea shook him to the core. And it was then that he got the idea.

He took his Bible and turned to a blank page in the back. On that page, he wrote down the names of twenty-four of his friends. He knew these guys. Like him, they were all in their early twenties. The idea that all of them wouldn't finish strong was unthinkable. Maybe Satan would pick off a few, but surely most of them would stick. These were guys who would be willing to die for Christ, if necessary.

I heard Bisagno tell this story a number of years ago. It got very quiet in the room when he began to tell the rest of the story.

"As the years have gone by, from time to time I have gotten a letter or a telephone call. And sadly, I have turned to the page in the back of my Bible and had to put a line through a name. I would always do that with such great sadness. The years have gone by and I am now fifty-three years old. Of the original twenty-four names in the back of my Bible, there are just three of us left."[2]

Twenty-four young men who were all in their early twenties. And thirty-two years later, there are just three of them still standing. The majority of those men had ruined their lives before they turned forty.

What will your life look like when you turn forty?

PACE IN THE RACE

Winston Churchill said, "It is always wise to look ahead, but difficult to look farther than you can see." It's tough to think about the finish line when it's fifty or sixty years away. The finish line is when you die. So if you're right around twenty, you probably have fifty or sixty years ahead of you before you hit the finish line.

It's hard to focus that far ahead. But it isn't that hard to see yourself at forty. That's one that you know is coming—and it's coming fast.

Could it be that John Bisagno's experience was unusual? I just turned fifty-six, and I am sad to say that it isn't.

Your early twenties are like a one-hundred-meter sprint. It seems like you're always running full speed. But life is not a sprint. It's a marathon. A marathoner has to think through his race; he has to pace himself; he has to prepare for the long haul.

I'm thinking of a very gifted woman who wrote books about family and marriage that were best sellers. She was speaking to thousands of women every year on how to be a woman of God. But her heart became drawn to another man—a Christian man who worked closely with her in her ministry. She ignored the advice in her own books and the Bible that she taught to thousands and left her husband and children. At the same time, she pulled the other man away from his wife and children. This gifted teacher of women managed to destroy two families in a matter of months. She violated the very principles that she taught. But she justified it by convincing herself that she had a right to be happy. When she said her marriage vows to her husband in the presence of God and her family, she never dreamed that she would do such a thing in her forties. But that's precisely what she did.

Allow me to relate one more story from *Finishing Strong* that underscores the point. You are aware, of course, of Billy Graham. Sixty years ago, there were three young evangelists who were shaking the world for Christ. Billy Graham was one of them. The year was 1945, and he was filling arenas and auditoriums as he preached the gospel with boldness and courage. You might have seen Billy Graham on television and noticed that he was old and frail. By the time you read these words, perhaps he has gone on to be with the Lord.

But sixty years ago he was a dynamo. He spoke at an average rate of 275 words a minute. At the age of twenty-seven, he was speaking to thousands.

But at the same time there were two other young evangelists having as great an impact as Billy Graham. They, too, were in the their mid-twenties, and they were both preaching to thousands upon thousands.

The first was Chuck Templeton. Like Billy Graham, he worked with Youth for Christ. He was filling the same arenas with thousands just like Graham. Hundreds were coming to know the Lord. Templeton was a commanding presence in the pulpit. Even though he was just barely twenty-five, he preached with an authority and a boldness that was beyond his years. He was a powerful communicator and the hand of God was obviously on his ministry.

In the South, there was another powerful young evangelist by the name of Bron Clifford. He also was a powerful and dynamic force in the pulpit for Christ. Thousands were coming out to hear him, so many that people would line up hours before the service began to make sure they got a seat. Clifford was packing churches and auditoriums from Florida to Texas. People were saying that he was the greatest preacher since the apostle Paul.

"At the age of twenty-five young Clifford touched more lives, influenced more leaders, and set more attendance records than any clergyman his age in American history. National leaders vied for his attention. He was tall, handsome, intelligent, and eloquent. . . . It seemed as if he had everything."[3]

In 1945 these three young men, Graham, Templeton, and Clifford, were the talk of American Christianity. I have a question for you. If these young guys were so famous, how come you've only heard of Billy Graham? Why aren't the names Chuck Templeton and Bron Clifford household names as well?

In 1950, Chuck Templeton walked away from Christ. Templeton decided that he did not believe that Christ was who He claimed to be. And the reason he doubted the claims of Christ was that he'd started attending a liberal seminary that taught that the words of the Bible could not be trusted. If the Bible could not be trusted, then Christ could not be trusted. Just five years after being considered perhaps the preeminent evangelist in America, Templeton denied Christ and became a broadcaster in Canada.

Templeton started strong in his twenties but denied Christ by the time he was thirty.

What about Bron Clifford, the young fireball preacher in the South?

Nine years later, in 1954, Clifford was dead. His body was found in a cheap hotel room in Amarillo, Texas. He died an alcoholic from cirrhosis of the liver. But long before he died, he had walked away from his family. He and his wife had two sons, each of them handicapped with Down syndrome. He left his wife when it seemed the pressure of caring for the children became too great. He lost his integrity and his right to preach. He began selling used Chevrolets and drinking heavily.

In his day, this young powerful communicator was without equal in proclaiming the truth. He just couldn't apply the truth. The "greatest preacher since the apostle Paul" died at thirty-five after walking away from not only his wife and children, but from Christ.

Bron Clifford started strong with Christ in his twenties. But he turned his back on everything he had preached by the time he was thirty-five.

I wish I could tell you that Templeton and Clifford are the exception. But they are not. I could tell you at least three hundred stories of men and women I have known of personally who started strong with Christ in their twenties, but ruined their lives by forty.

I must honestly tell you, it has put the fear of God in me. I hope these true accounts do the same for you.

Here is the burning question: What happened to these individuals? Where did they go wrong?

Something went wrong in their thinking.

They forgot that every action has a reaction.

They ignored the truth that every choice brings a consequence.

The logic of cause and effect was lost to them as they pursued the temptation that seemed so promising.

And as a result they were tragically defeated somewhere close to the halfway marker in the race.

You are just starting the race.

The wisdom that is necessary to run the race isn't learned overnight.

That's why He's willing to give you another start.

If you want to ruin your life by forty, never consider God's purpose for your existence.

"By You I have been sustained from my birth;
You are He who took me from my mother's womb."
PSALM 71:6

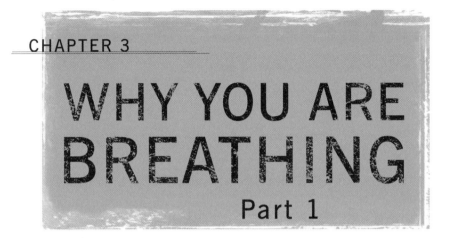

CHAPTER 3

WHY YOU ARE BREATHING
Part 1

Why do you exist?

This is the central question of your life.

Have you ever sat down and really thought about this?

Why are you alive right now? For thousands of years, the world went on without you. You weren't. But now you are. And you will always be. Did you ask to exist? Did you go online and fill out an application to begin the process of existing?

Why are you walking the earth now instead of three hundred years ago or one hundred years in the future?

The gnawing desire of every human being is to know the purpose of his existence deep in his heart. Unless you settle this question you are simply wasting your life. And all your efforts and achievements will mean nothing when you get to the finish line.

But to know why you exist, you can't start with yourself. You have to start with God. When someone doesn't start with God, they get selfish. And when self becomes the center of your life, then you are well on your way to ruining your life by forty.

THE PRICE OF BEGINNING WITH SELF

Some of you reading this look back on your childhood years with great gratitude to your parents. But many of you have gone through deep pain in your growing-up years.

I will never forget the day when one of our daughter's friends came to our house completely dressed in black. I had come to know her fairly well, since they were both in a lot of school activities together and she had been attending a Bible study in our home. But always before she had been vivacious and quite normal. This time, her blonde hair was dyed black, her fingernails and lipstick were black, and she seemed withdrawn. I pulled my wife aside in the kitchen and asked if it was the same girl. "Yes," she said. "You probably haven't heard. Her father has just left her mother and is filing for divorce."

Eventually, I learned that her father, a pastor on the staff of a local church, had become involved with another woman in the church and had walked away from the Lord and his family. It suddenly made sense why this young woman would dress in black; she was grieving over a death—the death of her family. Her relationship with the Lord also seemed to die with the death of her parents' marriage. Her family struggled to just survive from that point forward, and the driving force in this girl's life became the goal of never ever being dependent on a man again.

Off in his new world of self-fulfillment, this man was completely oblivious to the damage he had inflicted on the lives of his wife and children. But his sin, as James 1:14–15 tells us, will eventually lead him down to his own destruction. Why would someone kill his own family? Actually he killed two families, his own and the family of the woman he got involved with. This same man would never have entertained the idea of robbing a store or committing some other petty crime. But like the famous woman Bible teacher in the last chapter, he had no problem killing two families for his own happiness.

> If you want to know your **PURPOSE** and make your life count, then start with **God.**

Perhaps your dad came home and announced that he was leaving because he was in love with someone else. And without really caring about anyone in the family, he very calmly packed his things and left. As he left he assured you that everything would be all right. But it wasn't all right.

If your father did that, the big question is, *Why would he do such a horrible thing?* May I tell you the answer? He did it because he began with himself. And when people begin with self they get selfish. And that selfishness not only ruins them but the lives of everyone else around them. How can a father justify destroying his own family? Because he's selfish, and quite frankly, he doesn't care about anyone else other than himself and his own selfishness. There are severe consequences to be reckoned with when someone starts with self.

As I have talked with men who have abandoned their families, so many times they responded to me, "Don't I have a right to be happy?" The answer I always give them is, "No, you don't have that right." The real question they are asking is, "Don't I have a right to be selfish?"

If you want to know your purpose and make your life count, then start with God. If you want to have a godly home and a great marriage, then know up front that you can't start with yourself. You start with

Almighty God and His Word.

Don't let the sins of your father or mother keep you from knowing the true and living God. He will be your Rock.

BEFORE TIME BEGAN

So why do you exist? To answer requires going back before time existed. God existed before time. God the Father, God the Son, and God the Holy Spirit. Not only did He exist before time, but He created time. "All things came into being through Him, and apart from Him nothing came into being that has come into being" (John 1:3).

He is not only the Creator; He is the Ruler over all. He is the Sovereign Ruler. He has ordained all things, including your existence. He has declared the end from the beginning. Every being and event has been known and foreordained by God since before the foundation of the world (Isaiah 46:9–11), including the sacrifice of His very Son (1 Peter 1:20–21).

Think about it. God knew your name and my name before He shaped the universe. Such thoughts are mind-boggling; they are too high and too deep. To Jeremiah the prophet God said, "Before I formed you in the womb I knew you" (Jeremiah 1:5).

That's not only true of Jeremiah; it's true about you. He knew you before He made you.

Finally, God has spoken to us first through "prophets in many portions and in many ways," and "in these last days has spoken to us in His Son . . . [who is] the exact representation of His nature, and upholds all things by the word of His power" (Hebrews 1:1–3).

Now you've got to catch this. He knew you before He wove you together in your mother's womb. You exist by His will. But God not only creates, He speaks. Why has He spoken? So that we can know Him—so that *you* can know Him.

"He is there and He is not silent," wrote Francis Schaeffer. We can know Him, but we will never *comprehend* Him. "How unsearchable are His judgments and unfathomable His ways!" (Romans 11:33).

This God who created you and speaks to you is an absolutely awesome and magnificent God. He is not to be trifled with—you can know Him and receive His goodness and mercy, but only on His terms.

C. S. Lewis captures the awesome enigma of the nature of our God. In C. S. Lewis's *The Lion, the Witch, and the Wardrobe*, God's nature is described:

> "Is—is he a man?" asked Lucy.
>
> "Aslan a man!" said Mr. Beaver sternly. "Certainly not. I tell you he is the King of the wood and the son of the great Emperor-beyond-the-Sea. Don't you know who is the King of Beasts? Aslan is a lion—the Lion, the great Lion."
>
> "Ooh!" said Susan, "I'd thought he was a man. Is he—quite safe? I shall feel rather nervous about meeting a lion."
>
> "That you will, dearie, and no mistake," said Mrs. Beaver; "if there's anyone who can appear before Aslan without their knees knocking, they're either braver than most or else just silly."
>
> "Then he isn't safe?" said Lucy.
>
> "Safe?" said Mr. Beaver; "don't you hear what Mrs. Beaver tells you? Who said anything about safe? 'Course he isn't safe. But he's good. He's the King, I tell you."

He is the Lion, the Creator King, and no, He is not safe.

But He is incredibly good.

He has all power on heaven and on earth. He is holy and just, awesome and mysterious. He is to be reverenced and feared. And yes, He will judge those who violate His laws and spit upon His name. He will make right what is wrong and vindicate the weak and the helpless.

THE LION IS THE LAMB

This almighty Lion is also the sacrificial Lamb who laid down His life so that we might have it. He did this for you. He has demonstrated beyond doubt that He is good. He is faithful, merciful, and full of loving-kindness. His love and compassion are incomprehensible (Ephesians 3), so great that "neither death, nor life, nor angels, nor principalities, nor things present, nor things to come, nor powers, nor height, nor depth, nor any other created thing, will be able to separate us from the love of God, which is in Christ Jesus" (Romans 8:38).

In the same way, the Creator King has a plan for each one of us that is not safe—for it requires denying ourselves, taking up our cross, and following after Him (Matthew 16:24); but it is truly *good*—for He honors, blesses, and cares for those who honor Him (1 Samuel 2:30; Matthew 6). You have His word on it.

There is a word for this kind of sovereign love that God pours out upon His children. It's called *providence*. It's a term that we don't use anymore, and the loss of the word and its greatness is a tragedy. So what is this providence that will help you to understand why you exist?

Providence refers to God's management of what He created. That would include you. "His management of His creation is micro-management, concerned with and involved with the smallest details."[4] How do we know that God is a micromanager?

Wayne Grudem explains it very clearly:

Hebrews 1:3 tells us that Christ is "upholding the universe by his word of power." The Greek word translated "upholding" is *phero*, "carry, bear." This is commonly used in the New Testament for carrying something from one place to another, such as bringing a paralyzed man on a bed to Jesus (Luke 5:18), or bringing a cloak and books to Paul (2 Timothy 4:13). It does not simply mean "sustain," but has the sense of active, purposeful control over the thing being carried from one place to another. In Hebrews 1:3, [the grammar] indicates that Jesus is *"continually* carrying along all things," in the universe by the word of his power.

Similarly, in Colossians 1:17, Paul says of Christ that "in him all things hold together." The phrase "all things" refers to every created thing in the universe and the verse affirms that Christ keeps all things existing. . . . If Christ were to cease his ongoing activity of sustaining all things in the universe, then everything except the triune God would cease to exist.[5]

That means you and your iPod and everything else in the world would cease to exist if the Lord Jesus didn't keep it going. This is true and it is staggering. And it applies to all things. John Piper writes:

All things includes rolling dice (Prov. 16:33), falling sparrows (Matt. 10:29), failing sight (Ex. 4:11), financial loss (1 Sam. 2:7), the decisions of kings (Prov. 21:1), the sickness of children (2 Sam. 12:15), the suffering and slaughter of saints (1 Pet. 4:19; Ps. 44:11), the completion of travel (James 4:15), repentance (2 Tim. 2:25), faith (Phil. 1:29), holiness (Phil. 3:12–13), spiritual growth (Heb. 6:3), life and death (1 Sam. 2:6), and the crucifixion of Christ (Acts 4:27–28). From the smallest thing to the greatest, good and evil, happy and sad, pagan and Christian, pain and pleasure—God governs all for his wise, just and good purposes (Isa. 46:10).[6]

When He governs *all*, that means He governs you and all of the events of your life—including your very existence.

With that kind of magnificent power, aren't you glad that He is good? It was out of His goodness that He created you, and it is out of His goodness that He will give you everything you need at the precise moment you need it. That is providence. He will oversee your life at all times and provide for you. He is the reason that you are breathing. And He is the reason you keep breathing.

In Psalm 139, David is going to answer the question, *Why do I exist?* But he doesn't actually get to the answer until he gets halfway into the psalm. The first thirteen verses of Psalm 139 he spends contemplating the providence of God. That's why we have spent so much time laying the groundwork. It's pretty important to know why you exist. But what's even more important is to know the One who called you into existence.

THE INVISIBLE HAND

In Psalm 139:1–6, David writes:

(1) O Lord, You have searched me and known me.

David is saying that God is all knowing and has an intimate understanding of all His creation, including you. He knows absolutely everything about you. He knows more about you than you know about yourself.

(2) You know when I sit down and when I rise up;
You understand my thought from afar.

God knows you so well that He knows every move you make and every thought you think. He understands you, even when you don't understand yourself.

(3) You scrutinize my path and my lying down,
And are intimately acquainted with all my ways.

God intimately understands every experience, choice, and moment of your life, even when you are asleep. He knows your quirks and your uniqueness. He loves you—and get this, He likes you. When you have kids, you will love them and like them. And you will discipline them when they are disobedient. The Lord knows all of our ways and will give us what we need at the right time.

(4) Even before there is a word on my tongue,
Behold, O Lord, You know it all.

God even knows the thoughts you are going to think before you think them and put them into words. And He already knows every word you will speak for the rest of your life until the moment you die.

(5) You have enclosed me behind and before,
And laid Your hand upon me.

God sets His limits around you, guarding not only what is behind you, but also what is in front of you, and He puts His providential hand upon you. Your life is like a biography—actually, your life *is* a biography. Every biography breaks up into chapters, including yours. But God has also written chapters for your future that are as clearly marked as the chapters you've already been through. You just can't see them yet. You see, His hand really is on you. In your past, your present, and in your future.

(6) Such knowledge is too wonderful for me;
It is too high, I cannot attain to it.

When David gets done with this description of God, he is just flat-out overwhelmed. *"It is too high, I cannot attain to it."* David is just completely blown away by the greatness of God. He is astonished that God is that great and that concerned about everything in his life. It is so staggering that David cannot fully comprehend it. God is not like us.

- ♣ He's big—you're not.
- ♣ He knows all things—you're trying to pass calculus.
- ♣ He understands you intimately—half the time you can't figure yourself out.
- ♣ He has all power over the events of your life—you're weak even on steroids.
- ♣ He knows what's best—you're just guessing.
- ♣ His providential hand is upon you—you're just trying to get through the day.

David goes on to say in this psalm that God is everywhere, and that there is no escaping His presence. No one can hide from Him, even if we go to the bottom of the ocean or fly to the moon. His invisible hand is there, laying hold of us (verse 10).

By the end of verse 12, we learn that God knows all, sees all, and is everywhere. Nothing escapes His notice. All is known by Him even before it occurs. And never once does He take His hand off our lives. In other words, He's got you covered.

That's why I enjoy reading biographies. We all know that a biography is the true story about someone's life and work. But lately I've come to view biographies from a different angle. In the last few years, I've read close to a hundred biographies of people who have made a difference in this world. And I have found myself struck by the remarkable "hand of God" that weaves through their lives. What appears to be chance or an accident inevitably turns out to be the very thing that God has used to move them into the place where He could use them. That's true in your life as well.

The biography of a child of God is a story of providence.

Providence is that unseen hand of God, *the bringing together of God's sovereignty and His goodness upon your life.*

HARD TIMES AND PROVIDENCE

Winston Churchill was the man who saved England from Hitler's demonic quest to conquer the world. That was undoubtedly Churchill's greatest work. But when Winston Churchill was twenty-four, he knew nothing about World War II that would take place forty-one years in the future.

All Churchill knew at twenty-four was that he was a prisoner of war in a Boer detention center deep in South Africa. He decided, along with two other soldiers, to escape. He managed to walk out of the prison, but his friends were detained. Unfortunately, his friends possessed the compass and the map, and Churchill was unsure of what direction he should go.

"Armed with seventy-four pounds sterling, four slabs of chocolate, and a few biscuits he faced three hundred miles of hostile territory populated by people whose language he did not understand. Beyond that, within days his description and news of the reward for his capture would be known throughout the country."[7]

He was a fugitive and his picture was prominently posted on wanted posters across the region. He hopped a train and slept among sacks of coal. Then he waited for another train to come, but it never did. After several days, he was hungry and thirsty and hiding in a secluded ravine near the train tracks. As he began to walk the tracks, he discovered that each bridge was manned by Boer soldiers. There was no way out. Churchill became disoriented and desperate. Off in the distance, he saw the lights of what appeared to be a mining camp.

Completely spent, he had no option but to approach a small house on the outskirts of the mining settlement. He knocked on the door and a man answered. The man had a loaded pistol, and it was aimed at Churchill. Trying to bluff his way out of the situation, young Churchill finally blurted out the truth to the armed man. The man put down the pistol and replied in English, "Thank God you've come here. It is the only house for twenty miles where you would not have been handed over. But we are all British here and we will see you through."[8]

Within weeks Churchill was back in England. The newspapers had picked up the story of his amazing escape, and he immediately became a national hero. Churchill knew that God had answered his prayers. If he had gone to any other house other than the one he chose, he would have ended up right back at that Boer prison camp . . . at best. But the providence of a good God had delivered him.

If you think about it, you can clearly see the hand of God as you look back over your life. Were you riding in a car that flipped four times and you walked away from it? Did your mother consider having an abortion when she was pregnant with you—but she didn't? Did you pass senior math in high school and graduate by a decimal point? Even in the hard things, you can see the hand of God. The psalmist David spent much of his early years running for his life from a king who had turned his back on God. Yet at every turn, God was there. He gave him true friendship, escape from death, and provision for his needs. David wrote in Psalm 23: "Even though I walk through the valley of the shadow of death, I fear no evil, for You are with me. . . .You prepare a table before me in the presence of my enemies."

I said it earlier and I want to say it again, because it is critical that you capture this concept in your heart. Just as in a biography, your life breaks up into chapters. And David is telling us that God has enclosed you *behind*—meaning those chapters that you have already come through. But He has enclosed you *before*—meaning those future chapters that lie ahead of you.

In other words, God is the safety net beneath you as you walk through life. You are not just wandering through life. You are going somewhere. There is a plan for your life. You're not alive by chance or accident. You exist by a predetermined, providential plan of Almighty God. And the plan that He has for you is greater than anything you could ever come up with for your own life.

He knows what He is doing. He's looking to see if you are willing to trust Him with your life to discover what He has already written for you.

THE NET

Karl Wallenda didn't have a safety net. Wallenda was the greatest high-wire aerialist of the twentieth century. He was the head of the family circus act "The Flying Wallendas." The thing that set them apart from other high-wire acts is that they refused to use a net. In 1962 at a circus in Detroit at thirty-five feet above ground, the Wallendas were performing their famous seven-person chair pyramid. Four men stood on the high wire, yoked by shoulder bars. Above them stood two more, again yoked by a shoulder bar. At the pinnacle was a woman, sitting and standing on a chair! On this day, the front man faltered and the pyramid collapsed, leaving the rear anchorman alone standing on the wire. Karl and his brother fell to the wire from the second level. The girl on top landed on Karl, and he miraculously held her until a makeshift net could be brought in to catch her. The other three fell to the ground, and that night two of them died. The other, Karl's son, survived, though he was paralyzed from the waist down.

Amazingly Karl kept performing until in March of 1978 when at the age of seventy-three, while performing before a huge crowd in San Juan, Puerto Rico, he fell to his death. According to his wife, several months before, he'd had a premonition that he would fall. For three months, as he prepared for this, his most dangerous high wire act yet, all he seemed to be able to think about was the potential that he would fall. He even oversaw the installation of the tightrope on that fateful day, making sure all the wires were safe.

What killed Karl that day? His anxiety? His age?

What killed him was the fact that he had no net.

You have a net.

The providence of God is your net. If you fall, He will catch you, He will rescue you, He will restore you. And He will actually work the fall for your good (Romans 8:28).

Do you believe God is who He says He is? Do you grasp the significance of His invisible hand? The Lord God has enclosed you before and behind. He has already determined the moment of your death. And you can't die until that moment. When that day arrives, there's not one thing you can do to change it. "It is appointed for men to die once and after this comes judgment" (Hebrews 9:27). Until then, His hand will uphold you and lead you every second of your life.

We can get anxious about missing God's will. We can obsess over the potential for pain or disaster. Some of us worry ourselves sick, like Wallenda.

God is for you. He's on your team. He's your safety net. He is watching over you. He knows what you need and will provide it at the exact right moment. God is involved in every detail of your life, including your decisions, both good and bad, wise and unwise. If you make a bad choice, His providence is there to catch you.

Therefore, don't live in a state of constant anxiety. Anxiety-driven people are self-absorbed people who need to feel in control. It's a miserable way to live, and it is all wasted energy.

Don't misunderstand me. Anxiety is natural—just as is anger. It's what you do with anxiety and anger that counts.

Yes, you've got to think wisely and recognize the consequences of your choices. But there's a huge difference between thinking things through carefully and anxiously obsessing. "Tremble and do not sin; meditate in your heart upon your bed, and be still," said David (Psalm 4:4). You cannot be anxious and peacefully still at the same time. You are either one or the other. My friend Joe Aldrich is right. You can worship or you can worry. But you can't do both at the same time.

So take your anxiety to the Lord (Philippians 4), and rest in the net.

The truth is that you don't have the ultimate control over anything in your life anyway. He does. He absolutely does. "Do not be worried about your life," said the Lord, "for your Father knows what you need before you ask Him."

The antidote to anxiety is to do your part: Seek out God and His wisdom, and then make your decisions. Then you've got to let go, move forward, and trust in the net of His goodness and mercy.

Are you going through an especially difficult chapter of life? God is intimately acquainted with every circumstance of your life. And He's not wringing His hands. He's got a plan. He knows what your future holds, and if you belong to Him, He's not going to let go of you. He is your safety net. Hang in there with Him, and trust in His invisible hand. One day this chapter will end and a new one will begin. That day could be tomorrow. You don't know. But He knows.

> The **ANTIDOTE** to anxiety is to do your part: Seek out God and His **wisdom,** and then make your decisions.

So what is the question?

The question is, *Why do you exist?*

We haven't fully answered that question.

We had to start with God.

Now let's take a closer look at you.

If you want to ruin your life by forty, refuse to take responsibility for your choices.

"You are His picked, culled, prime instruments which He will make use of to carry on His best and greatest work against His worst and greatest enemies in these latter days."

THOMAS BROOKS

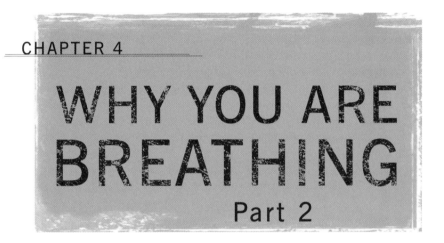

CHAPTER 4

WHY YOU ARE BREATHING

Part 2

You are not a mistake.

You are not an accident.

You were planned.

So why do you exist? God, the great Lion and Lamb, the King and Savior, foreordained from before the foundations of the earth that you should exist.

But for what purpose did He create you?

Very simply, *He created you to do a work.*

And He went to great lengths to equip you to do it. He actually began to equip you for your life's work when He formed you in your mother's womb.

That's where David takes us next in Psalm 139.

SKILLFULLY WOVEN

In the first twelve verses of Psalm 139, David talks about God. Now in verses 13–16, he switches gears and answers the question, *Why do I exist?*

Specifically, he ponders how he was created. And he is overwhelmed at what he finds. Through David's eyes, we begin to fathom the absolute wonder of God's creation of you and me. This amazing portion of Scripture explains straight out why you exist physically right now and are walking the earth.

> *For You formed my inward parts;*
> *You wove me in my mother's womb.*
> *I will give thanks to You, for I am fearfully and wonderfully made;*
> *Wonderful are Your works and my soul knows it very well.*
> *My frame was not hidden from You,*
> *When I was made in secret,*
> *And skillfully wrought in the depths of the earth.*

Anyone who has ever taken a class in human physiology or anatomy knows what David is talking about. Our bodies are amazing machines. They cause us to stand in awe of the Creator. We are fearfully and wonderfully made. From your very conception, while you were yet hidden in your mother's womb, God was weaving you, *skillfully* shaping you, with the hands of a master craftsman.

So why are you short or why are you tall? Why do you have blue eyes instead of brown, and straight hair instead of curly hair? Why is your skin the color it is? Why are you quick on your feet, or quick with your mind? Why are some people gifted musicians, while others can't carry a tune in a bucket?

IN THE BEGINNING GOD CREATED

David didn't know about DNA. In fact it wasn't until the last century that scientists began to discover the great inner cosmos of deoxyribonucleic acid, the amazing human genome that makes each of us the unique humans that we are. But Watson and Crick, along with hosts of other scientists since them, have only been uncovering what God created. Do you think that your genetic code, encrypted by twenty-three chromosomes from your mom and twenty-three chromosomes from your dad, is sheer accident? If it is, then your life has no real meaning or purpose. You are just a piece of matter, brought into existence by mere chance, for no real purpose.

The Bible says God purposefully brought all things into existence, including the first man and woman, from whom came a human race of people, each one skillfully wrought in his or her mother's womb, and each one with a purpose for existence.

ONE SPERM AND ONE EGG

You are not here by chance. You exist because God ordained that, out of an average of 400,000,000,000 sperm produced by your father, and hundreds of eggs produced by your mother, one sperm would hit one egg at just the right time and bring you into existence.

Have you considered what the chances of your never even existing are? If that single sperm, which only existed once, had not collided with that particular egg, which also only existed once, it would have simply perished and you never would have been born.

Think a little further with me here.

What if your dad had married that cheerleader from high school that he had a crush on instead of your mom? Would you exist if he married the cheerleader? The answer is no, because the cheerleader didn't have the right egg for you to exist.

And what if your grandfather had married the girl from the farm next door instead of falling in love with your grandmother at the ice-cream social? What if your great-great-grandfather had decided to stay in Europe, instead of migrating to New England where he met your great-great-grandmother? Have you considered statistically what it took for God to get you here, down through the thousands of generations and centuries, all the way from Adam and Eve?

You are no accident.

And you are more than a double-helical arrangement of chromosomes. Much more.

God designed you with unfathomable detail. Your personality, your strengths and aptitudes, the way you think and speak and laugh. What makes you tick? I mean, what gets your heart pumping? Are you good with people? Do you thrive on helping the sick or the weak? Do you soar as a leader, teacher, a great team player? Do you love the outdoors? Or reading? Or art? Are you good with your hands? Are you sharp in a crisis? Are you skilled at understanding and helping emotionally wounded people? Where did this come from?

It didn't happen by chance. It all comes from the Lord.

So often we look at other people and wish we could be like them. But God doesn't want you to be that other person—God wants you to be you. He went to a lot of detail to bring you into this world. And He likes you the way you are.

Some of you women need to hear this. Don't let some glitzy, brushed, half-naked picture on the cover of last week's edition of a magazine determine how you feel about yourself. And don't let a wealthy, media-hungry suburb of Los Angeles dictate who you should be. If you do, you'll never be happy with yourself. Seriously, who do you know of in Hollywood who is truly happy? These people are to be pitied. They know very little about true happiness and how to find it. They should have no influence on you whatsoever.

Listen to Psalm 139. Stand back and be amazed at how wonderfully you are made.

You are here for a purpose, and you are wonderfully made to fulfill it.

DEAD AND ALIVE

Have you ever driven by a cemetery and seen a hand push up out of the turf? Then another hand comes up, and then the head, and after some struggle you see a man pull himself up out of the grave?

That's ridiculous. Why is it unbelievable? Dead men can't change their condition. They can't just decide to become alive. And neither can spiritually dead individuals.

Are you still with me? Good. There's something very important here that you're not going to hear very often. Not even in the church.

And that is the fact that, if you know Christ, it is no accident that you have given your life to Him. Not only is your birth the awesome work of God, but Paul tells us that your spiritual birth is also the awesome work of God.

When you came into this world, you were very much alive physically. But you were spiritually dead.

"And you were dead in your trespasses and sins," Paul says (Ephesians 2:1).

Not uninformed. Not asleep. Not unconscious. Dead.

That's a serious predicament. Can a dead person change his condition? Of course he can't. He's dead. You can't *will* yourself to be alive spiritually any more than you can will yourself to rise up physically from the dead.

Then if you have been "born again," as Jesus put it, how did you go from being dead to being spiritually alive? God made you alive.

"But God, being rich in mercy, because of His great love with which He loved us, even when we were dead in our transgressions, made us alive together with Christ," says Paul (Ephesians 2:4–5).

God touched your dead spiritual soul and gave you life.

He made you alive. Just like he made Lazarus alive.

Do you remember the day you came to realize that God loved you? Do you remember that moment or that series of moments in your life when you felt the heavy weight of your sin and that tug on your heart? Do you remember that desire to give your life to Him? That realization, that tug, came from God. He called you out and infused you with spiritual life.

Now here is a most remarkable teaching. Even your faith is a gift from Him: "For by grace you have been saved through faith; and *that* not of yourselves, it is the *gift of God*, not as a result of works, so that no one may boast" (verses 8–9).

What is the *gift* of God? Look back at that verse: *Grace* was a gift, your *salvation* was a gift, and even your awakening and exercising of *faith* was a gift—the whole ball of wax.

Recently an attractive, sharp young woman who was attending one of my conferences told me her story. It was a story of abuse and abandonment, of running away from home as a young girl and living on the streets, of being taken in by a famous person in Hollywood, of going from man to man, of two abortions. One day she walked into the wrong clinic to get her third abortion; it was a pregnancy center that showed her a sonogram of the little baby growing in her womb. It had never occurred to her that this was a little life she was carrying. She walked out of the clinic and decided to give this child a chance to live. Thrown out by her boyfriend, she barely survived the ordeal. A few years after the baby was born, she happened upon a local church. And it was there that she met Christ. She also met her future husband. I met her husband that day; he was a Christian man who treasured her and would not even kiss her until the day of their

> God has **A WORK** for you to do, which He has *already* prepared beforehand.

marriage. He wanted her to know he was not marrying her for her body. And I met her child, a good-looking young man now entering his teens.

As remarkable as her story was, I was struck by something else she said to me. She had recently been studying the book of Ephesians. "You know," she said, "when I learned about God's sovereign hand in my salvation, it changed my whole perspective. When I understood that He did it all, it was almost like being born all over again."

This is why it is called *amazing* grace. God gets the credit. Was her entering the wrong clinic an accident? Was this child of hers an accident? Was her introduction to Christ an accident? Was the tug on her heart and the infusion of faith that changed her life an accident? None of it was an accident. It all came from the hand of God upon her life.

If you know Christ, God brought you alive and drew you to Himself. Did you make the decision? Yes. But how were you able to make that decision? God enabled you.

And He did it because He has a work for you to do.

That's exactly what Paul tells us in the next verse.

"For we are His workmanship, created in Christ Jesus for good works, which God prepared beforehand so that we would walk in them" (verse 10).

God has a work for you to do, which He has already prepared beforehand. How will you discover this work and do it? That's what we will look at in detail in the next chapter.

But before we get to that, we've got to tackle an obvious question.

WORKING IT OUT

I know the question that is rumbling around in your head. You are wondering, *Where do my choices come in? What about my decisions that determine the direction of my life? Don't I have something to do with all this?* That's a great question, and yes, you do.

"Work out [or live out] your salvation with fear and trembling; for it is God who is at work in you, both to will and to work for His good pleasure," Paul writes in Philippians 2:12–13.

There it is in black-and-white.

The great mystery of God's work and our work. It is just as much a mystery as the mystery of Jesus, the God-man, or the mystery of God-inspired Scriptures that came from human pen.

To know God is to embrace great mystery.

"*Work it out*," says Paul, "for *God is at work* in you."

"*Follow me*," says Jesus, yet "no one can come to Me *unless the Father who sent Me draws him*" (John 6:44).

"*Faith*, if it has no *works*, is dead," says James (James 2:17).

I've known people who assume that faith means they just sit back passively and God will make everything happen. On the contrary, God works as we are *in motion*, wrestling with decisions, searching the Scriptures, getting out there in life and doing things with excellence and plain old sweat and hard work.

We make decisions.

We get up and go to work or decide to sleep in.

We walk down the aisle of a church and make a wedding vow.

We submit résumés in order to get a job.

We wrestle with pain and disappointment.

We learn to rest in God when the going gets tough.

We fall into pits.

We climb out.

You and I are called to flesh it out. Yet all the while, God is working in and for us.

WRAPPING YOUR MIND AROUND THE MYSTERY

It's really the tightrope all over again, isn't it?

You and I are here, stepping out, learning to balance, making mistakes, growing, healing, walking away from sin, falling down, continuing on the road. And God is also very much here, with His invisible hand and invisible net. And if you look, you can't miss Him.

"How God governs all events in the universe without sinning, and without removing responsibility from man, and with compassionate outcomes is mysterious indeed."[9]

My wife, Mary, and I attended the same seminary, and we were both helped by the perspective of Dr. Robert Cook.[10] One day in class, Dr. Cook drew a large circle on the board. He explained that the circle was God's sovereign preordained will. Then he took his pen and made a tiny dot within the large circle. That dot represented man's will. The point that he was making is that all of our choices and decisions are within the larger circle of God's sovereign will.

The implication of this is that God knows your choices before you make them. Furthermore, all the decisions of your life are incorporated into His sovereign plan—before you ever make any of them. They are your choices even as they are part of His plan.

CERTAINTY WITHOUT COMPULSION

The mysterious, sovereign working of God involves *certainty without compulsion*. Thomas Watson puts it this way:

> The fact of free agency confronts us with mystery, inasmuch as God's control over our free, self-determined activities is as complete as it is over anything else, and how this can be we don't know.[11]

All of God's plan is *certain* to come about—even the dot that represents your life and choices. But although those choices are certain, you don't make them out of compulsion. You make them *because you want to*.

We aren't robots that are preprogrammed to make certain choices. We are men and women who are told to choose between the good and bad in life.

Let me give you just a sampling of the choices that are put before you in the Scriptures. We are told to "seek first the kingdom of God" (Matthew 6:33NKJV); to fear the Lord because that "is the beginning of wisdom" (Proverbs 9:10); to build our houses on the rock of His Word (Matthew 7:25); to search the Scriptures so that we can find life (John 5:39); to pray, for we have not because we ask not (James 4:2); and to "flee immorality" (1 Corinthians 6:18).

You can do those things or you can decide not to do them.

It's entirely up to you.

But choices have consequences.

If we obey the Scriptures, we will receive God's blessing—if we ignore them, we will receive His discipline.

Wayne Grudem proposes a response to the mystery of God's sovereignty and our choices:

> It seems better simply to affirm that God causes all things that happen, but that he does so in such a way that he somehow upholds our ability to make willing, responsible choices, choices that have real and eternal results, and for which we are held accountable. Exactly how God combines his providential control with our willing and significant choices, Scripture simply does not explain to us. But rather than deny one aspect or the other (simply because we cannot explain how both can be true), we should accept both in an attempt to be faithful to the teaching of all Scripture.[12]

So as you make your way down the road trip of life, you can be sure that "the mind of man plans his way, but the Lord directs his steps" (Proverbs 16:9).

John Ryland's poem expresses it well:

Sovereign Ruler of the skies,
Ever gracious, ever wise,
All my times are in thy hand,
All events at thy command.

His decree who formed the earth
Fixed my first and second birth;
Parents, native place, and time,
All were appointed by him.

He that formed me in the womb,
He shall guide me to the tomb;
All my times shall ever be
Ordered by his wise decree.

Times of sickness, times of health,
Times of penury and wealth;
Times of trial and of grief,
Times of triumph and relief.

Times the tempter's power to prove,
Times to test the Savior's love;
All must come, and last, and end
As shall please my heavenly friend.

Plagues and death around me fly;
Till he bids, I cannot die.
Nor a single shaft can hit
Till the love of God sees fit.[13]

ALL THE TIME YOU NEED

God didn't create you just to hang out at Starbucks all day. He has a work for you to do. He's equipped you to do it. And He has given you the exact number of days in your life needed to do that work. That brings us back to Psalm 139:

> *In Your book were all written,*
> *The days that were ordained for me,*
> *When as yet there was not one of them.*
> *(Psalm 139:16)*

Did you know that you are immortal until your work is done? Until you finish the work that God has planned for your life, death cannot touch you.

The president of the United States has important work to do. That's why he goes nowhere without highly trained secret service agents who are committed to preserving his life.

You have an even greater security detail with you wherever you go. The angels of God have been assigned to you to protect you. They are with you, and they will never leave you. They have been assigned to their post, and you are it (see Hebrews 1:13–14). They ensure that nothing can take you until your mission is accomplished. You have a work to do. And He will lead you and enable you to accomplish it. Even in threatening circumstances, your safety is assured.

You may get wounded; you may get roughed up.

But you will not die until your work is done.

If you want to ruin your life by forty, neglect the gifts and strengths that God has put within you.

*"It is better to fail in originality
than to succeed in imitation."*
HERMAN MELVILLE

CHAPTER 5

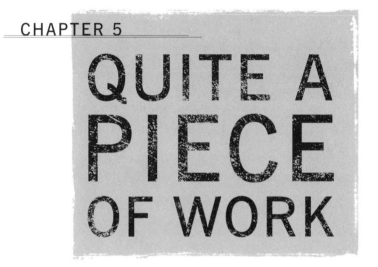

QUITE A PIECE OF WORK

There are two big issues that you face once you hit your twenties:

(1) What am I going to do?

(2) Who am I going to marry?

In this chapter we will deal with the issue of discovering the work you are called to do in this life. In the next two chapters, we will deal with the issue of finding a mate.

But for right now, let's talk about what you were created to do. And I'll give you a hint up front. It's about more than just making a lot of money.

LOVE WHAT YOU DO AND THE MONEY WILL COME

It is somewhat ironic that some of the most influential writing done over the last one hundred years from a Christian worldview came out of a pub in Oxford, England. And it wasn't just from the pen of one author. They had been meeting at the same pub on Thursday evenings for years. They were all scholars and writers. But most of all they were friends. They trusted each other. They understood each other. And they were very honest with one another. After dinner, they would all get comfortable and the question would be asked, "Does anyone have something to read?"

It was in this group that they would try out their new stuff on their friends to get their feedback. Everyone would listen and then give their opinion. It was in this small pub that J. R. R. Tolkien read aloud to his friends his manuscript of *The Lord of the Rings*. Around the same table, the members heard C. S. Lewis read to them his work, *The Lion, the Witch, and the Wardrobe*. Tolkien didn't think it was all that good, and he suggested to Lewis that he get to work on something else.

Undoubtedly, both Tolkien and Lewis would get a great laugh out of that now. They had no idea how far-reaching their books would be. And I'm sure they would have been stunned if someone had suggested that not only would they sell millions of copies, but millions of people around the world would watch their stories in theaters and in their homes.

It's astonishing to think that these two literary giants would meet twice a week for nearly thirty years in the back room of *The Eagle and Child Public House* and compare notes. Their informal group, which included R. E. Havard, Warren Lewis (brother of C. S.), Charles Williams, Owen Barfield, Nevil Coghill, Gervase Matthew, and Tolkien's son, Christopher, became known as "The Inklings."[14] They had different interests and professions, but they were all writers. They all loved to put their thoughts onto paper by way of ink.

What they had in common was a love for friendship, good ideas, and writing. Writing was their work. And they all did it because they loved it and they couldn't help themselves. It was just the way they were wired. You might say they felt *called* to it.

What about the man who built the pub in 1650? Did he have a gift for writing? I would imagine not. But he was gifted to construct buildings that would last for centuries. Is it possible that he loved to work with his hands and construct solid and comfortable homes and buildings that people could enjoy? He might even describe it to you as a calling.

What do you hope to do with your life?

What would you like your life to look like at forty? What would you love to do? What do you desire to do? Could it be that the Lord purposefully put those desires inside of you when He created you? Or does that sound too good to be true?

HIS WORKMANSHIP

You are quite a piece of work. It's clear from Psalm 139 that you exist physically because of God's will. Ephesians 2:8 makes it clear that we exist spiritually also by the will of God. But that's not the end of it. God gave us physical and spiritual life for a reason.

God has given you the **TOOLS** you need to **accomplish** the work He has for you.

You are unique. He gave you your bents, gifts, aptitudes, and skills. Those are your strengths. He also created you with your own set of weaknesses. And there are many strengths and gifts He purposefully did not give to you.

You don't have every strength and gift. There are some things you may even aspire to that He has not intended for you to do. You don't have every skill and every aptitude. You are not good at everything. But God has given you the tools you need to accomplish the work He has for you.

If you are not good with your hands, it's because the work He has for you to do does not require the skills of a craftsman. If you are not good with math, God's purpose for you will probably not involve engineering. If you don't have a bent toward mercy and compassion, you probably won't be called to be a nurse. The gifts and strengths He gives to us prepare us for our ultimate work that He has for us to do.

So don't walk around all day worrying about what you don't have. What do you possess from the good hand of the Lord? He ordained your gifts when He formed you in your mother's womb.

Count on this. He has a work for you to do that is very unique and vital. It doesn't mean that you will be famous, and it doesn't mean that you will be a celebrity. But it does mean that your life will be significant and purposeful.

Can I let you in on a secret? Over the years, I have had the somewhat unique experience of spending time with quite a few people who were famous. I'm talking about athletes, political leaders, ministry leaders, and musicians. For some reason the Lord has allowed me to have some time with these people who are very well-known. Now, I don't seek this and I don't broadcast it. I mention it for one reason. The one thing that all of these famous people have in common is that, down deep, they wish they weren't.

I have walked into restaurants with athletes, and every head in the room turned. That's why many of them don't ever go out to eat. They just can't get a night out with their family without being bothered.

They can't get on a plane and just sleep. Someone is always trying to get an autograph.

They can't pull into a gas station without having to autograph a paper towel.

I was meeting with one leader in his hotel room, and after a couple of hours he just wanted to walk down to the Coke machine and get a Diet Coke. Now if I told you his name, you would probably know it. He just wanted to walk down the hall, stretch his legs, and get a drink. But he had to look out of his door both ways down the hall to see if anyone was out there. He didn't want to get caught in the hall for five minutes and have to talk with people at that particular moment.

That's the downside of being famous. So don't desire it and don't seek it. And don't get conned into thinking that you need it in order to have a significant and meaningful life. I'm obviously not famous myself, but the experience of being around those who are has shown me that it can verge on being a curse. So do your work, enjoy your life, and go get a Starbucks, and be thankful that forty-seven people don't want your autograph and aren't spilling their lattes on your sweater.

God intends to use you for His glory whether you are famous or not. As Francis Schaeffer used to say, "There are no little people and there are no little places."

So how do you find what you were made for?

One of the most important jobs of a father and mother is to help their sons and daughters to discover what they are truly good at. Unfortunately, this often doesn't happen.

Ultimately, God will lead you to your unique niche in life. In fact, He will lead you all of your life, through the good and bad, just as He did with Joseph. But from the human side of things, let me give you some ideas to set you on a path of discovering how God has hardwired you.

Begin by realizing:

- ♣ You don't need to do what your father does.
- ♣ You don't need to do what your mother wants you to do.
- ♣ You don't need to do what other well-intentioned people think you should do.
- ♣ You need to follow what the Lord wants you to do.

And here's some great news: You will find great satisfaction in what the Lord wants you to do. Some people have this idea that God is only happy when He makes us miserable. So He will ask you to do something that is completely unrelated to your gifts and strengths. I think that is a very distorted view of God.

At times in life, He will test you and take you through hardship. And that may involve a season where you are seriously out of position in terms of your gifting and God-given motivations. When that happens you will be unhappy and frustrated. I have been through those times, and you will go through those times. Those are the times when God is testing us. Those times of testing are for a season, and they are for a reason. They don't last forever. But they serve a very important purpose in God's plan for your life. In the long run, if you will be teachable and obedient, they will actually work to prepare you for the work that He has for you to do.

A MOMENT OF CLARITY

You recall the story of Jane D'Esterre who faced a crisis at eighteen. Her great-great-grandson, Os Guinness, would face his own crisis years later. Only his was a crisis concerning his life work:

> In my early days of following Jesus, I was nearly swayed by others to head toward spheres of work they believed were worthier for everyone and right for me. If I was truly dedicated, they said, I should train to be a minister or a missionary. Coming to understand calling liberated me from their well-meaning but false teaching and set my feet on the path that has been God's way for me.
>
> I did not know it, but the start of my search lay in a chance conversation in the 1960s, in the days before self-service gas stations. I just had my car filled up with gas and enjoyed a marvelously rich conversation with the pump attendant. As I turned the key and the engine of the forty-year-old Austin Seven roared to life, a thought suddenly hit me with the force of an avalanche. This man was the first person I had spoken to in a week

who was not a church member. I was in danger of being drawn into a religious ghetto.

Urged on all sides to see that, because I had come to faith, my future must lie in the ministry, I had volunteered to work in a well-known church for nine months—and was miserable. To be fair, I admired the pastor and the people and enjoyed much of the work. *But it just wasn't me.* My passion was to relate my faith to the exciting and exploding secular world of the early 1960s Europe, but there was little or no scope for that in ministry. Ten minutes of conversation with a friendly gas pump attendant on a beautiful spring evening in Southampton, England, and I knew once and for all that I was not cut out to be a minister.[15]

Calling does not come through an audible voice of God. *Calling* simply refers to God's unique purpose and work for you. And it's already hardwired down deep into your soul. How do you recognize it? *When you think about it, you get motivated and excited. And when you get off track, you get discouraged or bored.*

What bores you? Whatever it is, don't pursue it as a career! Quit doing it. Marcus Buckingham teaches executives all over the country. Some of them make a lot of money in jobs that don't utilize their strengths. They are bored to tears. Buckingham's advice to them is simple: "Find out what you don't like doing and stop doing it."[16]

What excites you and gets you motivated? Whatever it is, you get excited and motivated because you are doing what God has hardwired you to do. Pursue it! Go after it!

When they were small, I used to read the following story to my three kids, Rachel, John, and Josh. Now they are all in their twenties and pursuing what God has put in their hearts. That's the point of the story:

Imagine there is a meadow. In that meadow there is a duck, a fish, an eagle, an owl, a squirrel, and a rabbit. They decide they want to have a school so they can be smart, just like people.

With the help of some grown-up animals, they come up with a curriculum they believe will make a well-rounded animal:

running,

swimming,

tree climbing,

jumping,

and flying.

On the first day of school, little br'er rabbit combed his ears, and he went hopping off to his running class.

There he was a star. He ran to the top of the hill and back as fast as he could go, and oh, did it feel good. He said to himself, "I can't believe it. At school, I get to do what I do best."

The instructor said: "Rabbit, you really have talent for running. You have great muscles in your rear legs. With some training, you will get more out of every hop."

The rabbit said, "I love school. I get to do what I like to do and get to learn to do it better."

The next class was swimming. When the rabbit smelled the chlorine, he said, "Wait, wait! Rabbits don't like to swim."

The instructor said, "Well, you may not like it now, but five years from now you'll know it was a good thing for you."

In the tree-climbing class, a tree trunk was set at a thirty-degree angle so all the animals had a chance to succeed. The little rabbit tried so hard he hurt his leg.

In jumping class, the rabbit got along just fine; in flying class, he had a problem. So the teacher gave him a psychological test and discovered he belonged in remedial flying.

In remedial flying class, the rabbit had to practice jumping off a cliff. They told him if he'd just work hard enough, he could succeed.

The next morning, he went to swimming class. The instructor said, "Today, we jump in the water."

"Wait, wait. I talked to my parents about swimming. They didn't learn to swim. We don't like to get wet. I'd like to drop this course."

The instructor said, "You can't drop it. The drop-and-add period is over. At this point you have a choice: Either you jump in or you flunk."

The rabbit jumped in. He panicked! He went down once. He went down twice. Bubbles came up. The instructor saw he was drowning and pulled him out. The other animals had never seen anything quite as funny as this wet rabbit who looked more like a rat without a tail, and so they chirped, and jumped, and barked, and laughed at the rabbit. The rabbit was more humiliated than he had ever been in his life. He wanted desperately to get out of class that day. He was glad when it was over.

He thought that he would head home, that his parents would understand and help him. When he arrived, he said to his parents, "I don't like school. I just want to be free."

"If the rabbits are going to get ahead, you have to get a diploma," replied his parents.

The rabbit said, "I don't want a diploma."

The parents said, "You're going to get a diploma whether you want one or not."

They argued, and finally the parents made the rabbit go to bed. In the morning the rabbit headed off to school with a slow hop. Then he remembered that the principal had said that any time he had a problem to remember that the counselor's door is always open.

When he arrived at school, he hopped up in the chair by the counselor and said, "I don't like school."

And the counselor said, "Mmmm, tell me about it."

And the rabbit did.

The counselor said, " Rabbit, I hear you. I hear you saying that you don't like school because you don't like swimming. I think I have diagnosed that correctly. Rabbit, I'll tell you what we'll do. You're doing just fine in running. What you need to work on is swimming. I'll arrange it so you don't have to go to running anymore, and you can have two periods of swimming."

When the rabbit heard that, he just threw up!

As the rabbit hopped out of the counselor's office, he looked up and saw his old friend, the Wise Old Owl, who cocked his head and said, "Br'er rabbit, life doesn't have to be that way. We could have schools and businesses where people are allowed to concentrate on what they do well."

Br'er rabbit was inspired. He thought when he graduated, he would start a business where the rabbits would do nothing but run, the squirrels could just climb trees, and the fish could just swim. As he disappeared into the meadow, he sighed softly to himself and said, "Oh, what a great place that would be. [17]

SWEET SPOT

What you're after is to find your sweet spot. If you dread going to work every day, you are probably not using your strengths and gifts that God has given you. If you are bored or always stressed out by what you are studying, you are off course. If you watch the clock at work all day long, you obviously are not in a job that utilizes your strengths.

But when you love going to work and can't wait to get there—that's a sure sign that you are homing in on your strengths.

When you are interested and energized and highly motivated in particular subjects, that's another clue that you are in your area of giftedness.

Usually, finding your sweet spot involves a process of experimenting and eliminating. This is a process that usually takes place throughout the twenties and thirties. It's sort of like a funnel that is wide on the top and narrow on the bottom. The older you get, the narrower the funnel should become. You are eliminating things you don't want to do and focusing in on what you do love. And as that process continues, you will find your sweet spot.

One word of caution: You must be realistic about your gifts. If you think you are highly gifted at something but in actuality you are not, you will be in for a lot of disappointment. Don't try to be what you aren't. If you are average at music don't plan on a music career. I think you get my point. You have to be very honest about who you are and how you are wired. And if you are open to input, people who love and care for you will give you honest input. They want the best for you as well.

This is a very short chapter, and finding your niche in life is a very big subject. So allow me to recommend a book that deals with this subject in a very practical and biblical way. The book is *Cure for the Common Life* by my friend Max Lucado. The subtitle of this excellent book is "Living in Your Sweet Spot." The book even contains a study guide that will help you to take the first steps in discovering how the Lord has hardwired you.

But here's the most important thing of all. Don't get focused on the work—get focused on Him. The work and career for some people can become an idol. Tell the Lord that you are willing to do anything and go anywhere. And if you say that, you should mean it from your heart. And then watch Him lead and navigate you to the work that He has for you. You will encounter setbacks, heartbreaks, delays, and blocked doors in the process. But in His perfect time He will show you His goodness, and you will realize that those setbacks and sorrows actually were part of the necessary process to prepare you for the work. I think I said that earlier in this chapter. But it is so important, I needed to say it again.

He is the One who has ordained the good works of your life. So seek Him. And don't seek Him third or fourth on your list of priorities. Put Him first in your life (Matthew 6:33–34), and follow Him in obedience.

Mark this down. If you want to walk in the good works that He has ordained for your life—if you want to avoid ruining and shipwrecking your life, then *obey* Him. If you do that, your purpose in life will not elude you and neither will His awesome favor.

Jesus said to His disciples, "Follow Me." They obeyed and followed Him. He says the exact same thing to you: "Follow Me." So do it with your whole heart and you will discover why you were born.

EVERY CALLING IS HONORABLE

God knows your future. God has a work for you to do. God's plan for you may be that you become an architect, a welder, a teacher, or a stay-at-home mom like Susannah Wesley.

Susannah Wesley had nineteen children, and two of her sons, John and Charles, along with their friend George Whitefield, were used by God to bring about revival in the eighteenth century. The spiritual revolution started by these men helped prevent England from embracing the chaos and anarchy happening in the French Revolution. Does that mean that her other seventeen children weren't equally valuable? Absolutely not. Ten of her nineteen children died in infancy before the age of two. Can you imagine such grief? Nine of her children lived to adulthood. All were equally valuable, significant, and important to Almighty God and to their mother and father. But they were all different and called to do different things in life.

Instead of nineteen kids, you may just have one. That child could end up in a wheelchair, an instrument of God's grace in ways you would never expect. Or he could wind up teaching millions of parents how to raise their children, as Myrtle Dobson's son, James Dobson, has done. He wound up teaching many principles he learned from his mother on the radio, in his books, and in his video series, to countless millions. But it all started with a gifted and creative woman staying at home with her child and teaching him.

Motherhood is a calling that much of the world mocks. But God thinks very highly of it.

Philip Anschutz made millions drilling for oil. Then he turned to railroads and laid fiber optic cable all over America. At the age of sixty-six, this committed Christian continues to narrow his focus. In a recent speech, he explained his motivation: "Four or five years ago I decided to stop cursing the darkness—I had been complaining about movies and their content for years—and instead to do something about it by getting into the film business."[18]

He knows that he is gifted at business, so he is taking his billions and investing them to influence popular culture. He has been buying newspapers across the nation, and he owns the largest chains of movie cinemas in the country.

His next decision was to make the movies that go into the theatres. Philip Anshutz is the man behind the movie, *The Lion, the Witch, and the Wardrobe*. That's why the British news magazine, *The Economist*, recently ran an article on him titled, "God's Media Mogul." The byline reads, "Philip Anschutz, an oil and telecoms billionaire, wants to bring morals to Hollywood."[19]

C. S. Lewis wrote books. He didn't drill for oil and he didn't make movies. But God gifted Philip Anschutz to do precisely that.

God created Susannah Wesley, John Wesley, Charles Wesley, George Whitefield, and Myrtle Dobson for a specific work. God also called everyone who has worked alongside them, including fathers who provided for those mothers and took their role as fathers seriously, and accountants, attorneys, communication experts, administrators, ad infinitum. God created the teachers who influenced and trained all of these people. God created the mentors who quietly modeled character and discipled them.

He has a work for you to do.

Stay with your gut and stay with your desires and interests.

Don't go after something just for the money.

Don't do it for recognition. Who cares what the world thinks?

Go after it because you love it, you're good at it, and you're highly motivated.

Go after it for the primary purpose of glorifying God.

The closer you get to forty, the more your work will come into focus. Ideally, during your twenties and thirties the Lord will get you ready for *even more* fruitful and productive years from forty to seventy.

As God leads you and develops you, He will test you. He will test your obedience and your character. Make sure that you pass those tests. Don't touch sin with a ten-foot pole. Work hard and let Him promote you.

And somewhere around forty, as you have been proven and tested, you may experience what Dr. Robert Clinton calls *convergence*.[20] Convergence is a time in your life where, after intense preparation, including successes and failure, and many testings, God brings you into a place in life where your strengths are maximized and your weaknesses are covered.

If I were you, I would pray for that.

Pray that God will put you in your sweet spot to accomplish His good work for His glory.

And when you do, you will one day look around and think to yourself, *This is what I was created to do.*

And you will be right.

If you want to ruin
your life by forty,
get sexually involved
before marriage.

*"To marry a woman for her beauty
is like buying a house for its paint."*
ANONYMOUS

CHAPTER 6

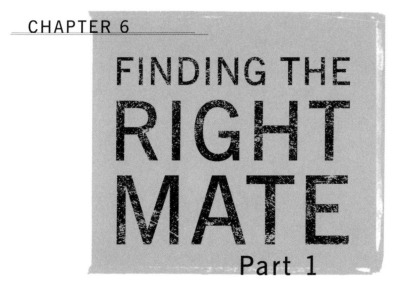

FINDING THE RIGHT MATE
Part 1

The most critical decision that you will ever make concerns Jesus Christ and whether or not you will follow Him from your heart all the days of your life.

The second most important decision of your life is who you are going to divorce.

Perhaps you were thinking that the second most important decision of your life is who you will marry. It used to be that people got married for life until one of them died. It was that way for thousands of years. But over the last forty years, our culture has shifted from a culture of lifelong marriage to a culture of convenient divorce. So you've got to decide before you get married the kind of commitment you are willing to make and the kind of commitment you are looking for from your spouse. Will you marry for life or will you marry for as long as it is convenient and easy?

Things have gotten so bad in our nation that it's actually easier to divorce your spouse than it is to fire someone who works for you. So before we discuss the ground rules for finding the right mate, we should discuss whether or not divorce is an option in the back of your mind as you approach marriage.

Did you know that the divorce rate among evangelical Christians is slightly higher than the divorce rate among non-Christians?

That is an astonishing statistic.

When you get married, you will make some vows. The vows normally go like this:

> *For better or worse,*
> *Richer or poorer,*
> *In sickness and in health,*
> *Till death do us part.*

Divorced Christian couples said those vows to one another. But somebody didn't mean what they said. Those vows were simply words. They were syllables that were mindlessly uttered without any heart behind them. Some couples set a date, buy a dress, rent a tuxedo, invite their families and friends to watch them as they say their vows to one another. But if there is no commitment behind the words, the whole thing is a sham.

Everyone wants to have a great a marriage. But it takes a tremendous commitment to have a solid marriage. In my book *Point Man,* I tell the story of the Spanish explorer Hernando Cortés. When Cortés and his men landed in the harbor at Veracruz, they began their journey into the new country. Suddenly one of the men called out, *"Fire!"*

As the men turned back to his voice, they saw the smoke coming from their ships. Not only was smoke coming from the ships, fire was engulfing their vessels and their way home.

They were shocked to find out the fires had been set at the command of their leader, Hernando Cortés. By burning the ships, Cortés cut off any hope of returning to Spain. The men did not know what awaited them as they entered Mexico. But now there was no enemy that could turn them back because there was no way to get back. Cortés had burned the ships. Now they had no alternative except to move forward.

The reason that Christian couples get divorced is that someone in the marriage didn't burn their ships. For many people, including professing Christians, commitment has been redefined to mean that they will stay in this relationship as long as it's personally convenient to do so. But that's not commitment. That's a fraud.

ARMED ROBBERY

I have a question for you. Is armed robbery an option for you if you run out of money? If your Visa bill comes in $300 higher than you expected, does it ever enter your mind to take a gun and stick up the local gas station? The reason you don't consider such an option to find $300 is simple. You have removed armed robbery as an option in your life.

Why don't you do that with divorce? Put divorce in the same category as armed robbery. It's not an option and it doesn't exist. In other words, when you get married, burn your ships.

The reason the vows say "for better or worse" is because you and your spouse will have both. There's no getting around it. You see, anyone can be committed when it's better—but the test of commitment is when it's worse. That's when commitment rises to the surface.

Anyone can be committed when it's richer. It's easy to be committed when you're both working and you don't have kids yet. It's easy being committed when you've got two salaries and you're able to buy a house and fix it up. It's easy to be committed when you can take a nice vacation together. Anybody can be committed when the money's flowing and life is good. But the test of commitment is when you start a business and it fails. Anyone can be committed when it's richer—but a real test is when you're just trying to survive financially.

Anyone can be committed when there's health. But a test of commitment is the loss of health. There is no guarantee that you or your spouse will always enjoy physical and emotional health. Sometimes depression hits an individual, and they just can't pull out of it. So what do they need from you in a time like that? They need commitment. What does your spouse need when they are going through chemotherapy? They need you to be committed in sickness.

If **DIVORCE** is an option for you, then **don't** get married.

And if you've burned your ships, and if you've removed divorce as an option, you will be there. That's how it's supposed to work. That's the only way it works.

If divorce is an option for you, then don't get married. If you go into a marriage thinking that divorce is an option if things get real tough, then guess what. You will get divorced. The reason that you will get divorced is that every marriage goes through difficult times.

But if you go into marriage thinking that divorce is not an option and you marry someone who shares that same perspective, then you can get married and stay married until one of you dies.

Before you consider marriage, you have to decide what you believe about divorce. That's one of the ground rules. But there are three more that are vitally important.

LAYING OUT THE GROUND RULES

It's time to make a list. We just went over the first ground rule, but there are three more right behind it. If you desire to follow Christ for the rest of your days and serve Him, then there are some ground rules that should be in place as you consider finding a mate for life. The second ground rule is for men and the third is for women. Ground rule number four applies to both.

1. *Remove divorce as an option before you marry.*
2. *Keep your cotton-pickin' hands to yourself.*
3. *Don't act or dress cheap.*
4. *Christians only marry Christians.*

Keep Your Cotton-Pickin' Hands to Yourself

I live in Texas and people around here say things like cotton-pickin'. You won't find cotton-pickin' in the Bible. But you certainly find the essence of ground rule number two in Scripture. Check out 1 Thessalonians 4:1-8.

> *Finally then, brethren, we request and exhort you in the Lord Jesus, that as you received from us instruction as to how you ought to walk and please God (just as you actually do walk), that you excel still more.*
>
> *For you know what commandments we gave you by the authority of the Lord Jesus.*
>
> *For this is the will of God, your sanctification; that is, that you abstain from sexual immorality; that each of you know how to possess his own vessel in sanctification and honor, not in lustful passion, like the Gentiles who do not know God; and that no man transgress and defraud his brother in the matter because the Lord is the avenger in all these things, just as we also told you before and solemnly warned you.*

For God has not called us for the purpose of impurity, but in sanctification. So, he who rejects this is not rejecting man but the God who gives His Holy Spirit to you.

That's very straight and to the point. It's very clear that there is to be no sexual immorality before or during marriage. The word here translated "sexual immorality" was used in New Testament times for any kind of sexual sin.[21] So that covers everything from mutual masturbation to oral sex to sexual intercourse to homosexuality and beyond.

If there is no sexual immorality permitted before you get married, then what is permitted in the physical relationship? In other words the big-time question is, *How far can we go?*

The answer to that is that if you know Christ, the Spirit of God lives within you. This Spirit of God, this third person of the Trinity who is fully and completely God, what is He called in this passage? Is He called the Loving Spirit? Is He called the Sovereign Spirit or the Truthful Spirit? He is all of those things, but that's not what He is called. He is the *Holy* Spirit. Holiness means moral purity. So this Holy Spirit who lives in you will let you know when you cross the line of moral purity.

Guys, if you're not married, then you are expected to honor "the younger women as sisters, in all purity" (1 Timothy 5:2). Your girlfriend is not your wife. You are not free to be sexually involved with her. She is your sister in Christ. So treat her with purity.

So who's dating your future wife right now? Maybe it's you. But it's possible that you have not yet met the woman you are going to marry. She may be halfway across the country or on the other side of your campus. Let's say that she's dating some other guy right now. Now here's the question. How do you want that guy to treat your future wife? Well, that's pretty clear, isn't it?

Would it send you off the roof if he held her hand? Probably not.

What if they kissed? Would that cause you to round up a posse and go after the guy? Well, that depends on how he is kissing your future wife. And where he is kissing her.

Maybe the woman you're going out with is going to be someone else's wife. Then why don't you treat her the way that you would like your wife to be treated by the guy who is dating her?

Maybe some of you guys still aren't getting this. Maybe you played too much football without a helmet. So let me spell it out for those who still may not get it when it comes to how far you can go.

No breasts.

How's that for being clear?

When you are fondling a woman's breasts, you have crossed the line of moral purity. From here on out, your line in the sand is no breasts. If you go to KFC, you don't even order a breast. That's how committed you are to this principle.

Do you want some guy touching your future wife's breasts? Then don't you touch the breasts of a woman that you are not married to. So what do you do if you have touched her breasts or had oral sex or even sexual intercourse?

You repent of this sin before the Lord Jesus and you stop before it goes any further. You take this to the Lord and tell Him what you've done and you vomit up your sin. That's what repentance is. It's turning away from the foulness of sin and going the other direction. It was Thomas Watson who said that genuine repentance is the vomiting of the soul. Fake repentance justifies sin, rationalizes sin, and minimizes sin. But authentic repentance does none of those things.

DON'T ACT CHEAP

If you belong to Christ, you shouldn't act cheap or dress cheap. You should dress modestly. Does that mean you have to dress like a pilgrim that just got off the *Mayflower*? Of course not. You should dress with style. Just don't dress cheap. Women, don't expose your breasts by what you wear. How you dress says something about your heart and how you view yourself.

How you dress sends a message about you to guys. If you dress like Paris Hilton, some guy is going to think that he can take you out and then sleep with you at the Hilton. You don't want to send that signal.

Don't let some guy touch you just because he says he loves you. If he loved you he wouldn't be trying to take you into sin.

First Corinthians 6:15–20 is for men and women:

Do you not know that your bodies are members of Christ? Shall I then take away the members of Christ and make them members of a prostitute? May it never be!

Or do you not know that one who joins himself to a prostitute is one body with her? For He says, "The two shall become one flesh."

But the one who joins himself to the Lord is one spirit with Him.

Flee immorality. Every other sin that a man commits is outside the body, but the immoral man sins against his own body.

Or do you not know that your body is a temple of the Holy Spirit who is in you, whom you have from God, and that you are not your own?

For you have been brought with a price: therefore glorify God in your body.

Maybe your father didn't tell you how valuable you really are. Perhaps he didn't treat you as though you were valuable. The Lord Jesus thinks you are so valuable that He died for you.

The story is told of a famous writer who was attending a dinner party of wealthy people in London. He was seated next to a beautiful woman. In the middle of their conversation, he leaned over to her and whispered, "Would you sleep with me tonight for $10,000?" She nodded to him that she would.

He whispered again, "How about fifty dollars?"

Thoroughly insulted, she said to the writer, "Fifty dollars! What do you think I am?

"We've already established that," replied the man. "Now we are simply negotiating."

It's been said that every man and woman have their price. Everyone, it is thought, can be bought. But the Lord Jesus is looking for those who can't be bought. He's looking for young women who can't be bought because they have already been bought. And they were bought with the price of His own blood.

When you understand how valuable you are to the Lord Jesus it frees you up to never act or look cheap again.

I know of a woman who was raised in a horrible background of abuse and immorality. At the age of fifteen, she was nothing short of stunning. She found herself as a high-priced call girl in a major city. Before she was eighteen, she was sleeping with men for $10,000 a night.

Today she is a wife and a mother. She serves with her husband on the mission field. She loves her life. She never thought with her background that she could have a husband who would love her unconditionally. But when she turned to the Lord, a radical transformation took place. "Therefore if anyone is in Christ, he is a new creature; the old things passed away; behold, new things have come" (2 Corinthians 5:17).

She thought she was condemned to live a life of cheap vulgarity and easy money. But when she turned to the Lord she found not condemnation, but mercy and forgiveness. She can't believe the life that God has given her. But that is what He does. He is a great God.

CHRISTIANS ONLY MARRY OTHER CHRISTIANS

In Matthew 7:24–29, Jesus talked about the foolish man who built his house on the sand. When the storms came his house was washed away. But then Jesus spoke of the man who built his house upon the rock. When the storms showed up his house withstood the test. The point is simply this: What you build upon is extremely important. It can literally be an issue of life and death.

Houses have foundations. A house is only as strong as its foundation. You've seen on the evening news million-dollar homes on a hillside sliding down into the ocean. That's ultimately a foundation issue.

> If you love **CHRIST**, why in the world would you **marry** someone who doesn't?

Marriages also have foundations. Psalm 127 declares that "unless the Lord builds the house, they labor in vain who build it." The context of Psalm 127 and 128 is the family. It's clear that the ones building a house are a husband and wife. But if they are not committed together to the Lord as they build a marriage, they already have a major breach in their foundation.

If you love Christ, why in the world would you marry someone who doesn't? You are already in conflict on the most important thing in your life. That's like buying a house on the San Andreas Fault in California that already has a three-foot-wide crack running through the living room. When a Christian marries a non-Christian, you are divided before you ever begin.

Second Corinthians 6:14–15 puts the truth right on the table:

Do not be bound together with unbelievers; for what partnership have righteousness and lawlessness, or what fellowship has light with darkness? Or what harmony has Christ with Belial, or what has a believer in common with an unbeliever?

So what does a believer have in common with an unbeliever? If you marry an unbeliever, what will you tell your kids about Jesus? If you marry an unbeliever, how will you make decisions together as a couple? You will pray and the unbeliever won't. That doesn't make a lot of sense.

Quite frankly, you are asking for trouble and misery if you violate this principle. So don't violate it.

If you smell gas in your kitchen, don't light a match to try and find the leak.

If you are attracted to someone who is not a Christian, get ahold of yourself and redirect your interest. Fight off the emotional attraction and walk away quickly. Don't give any consideration to the possibility that you might lead them to the Lord. God doesn't need you to do His work in their life. What He does want you to do is obey His Word concerning His instructions about marrying unbelievers. And here's a piece of logic for you: If you don't date unbelievers, you won't marry an unbeliever. Funny how that works.

HAPPILY MARRIED AT 40

It was Robert Schumann who said, "When I was a young man, I vowed never to marry until I found the ideal woman. Well, I found her—but, alas, she was waiting for the perfect man."

Perfection will be hard to find.

Perhaps it would be wiser to look for compatibility instead of perfection. If your focus is on finding a mate with whom you are compatible, you will give yourself a much higher probability of enjoying a satisfying and meaningful marriage at forty.

If you are compatible with someone, you fit with them. Or to put it another way, the two of you just "click."

If you are on AM and they are on FM, you are not compatible.

To be compatible is to be on the same frequency. It's the ability to understand and read someone—and they can do the same with you.

Very briefly, let me pass on some wisdom that was given to me nearly thirty years ago by Dr. Grant Howard.

Did you know that there are six key areas of compatibility that are part of any relationship? One of the goals before you get married is to find out how you fit with this other person in these six areas:

- *Intellectually*—interests and ideas you share in common; learning to think together, not always alike
- *Emotionally*—appreciating one another's emotional makeup; you both should feel understood by the other
- *Socially*—not embarrassed by the other in groups, comfortable with their speech and actions
- *Volitionally*—learning to make decisions together
- *Spiritually*—you are both seeking the Lord together and obeying His Word
- *Physically*—appropriately expressing the affection of your heart

Now here's an extremely important point. To find out if you are compatible with an individual in these areas, how many of those areas are discovered by touching? The answer is one, and it's obviously the physical.

How many of those six areas are developed by talking? The answer is five. You find out if you are compatible with someone intellectually, emotionally, socially, volitionally, and spiritually by talking.

That's five for talking and one for touching.

Now watch this logic. Therefore, I would conclude that before you are married, a relationship should be characterized by a maximum of talking and a minimum of touching.

Does that not make sense?

Sure it does. It made sense when Dr. Howard said it thirty years ago, and it makes sense now.

What happens when a couple gets real involved physically? They get deceived into thinking that they are very close. But they are not close. They are close physically. But they are not close volitionally. Volition is the ability to choose, to decide. So if you marry this person, will you use credit cards or not? Will you put your kids in public schools or homeschool them?

It's amazing how many couples are very intimate and very close physically—but they are miles apart in the areas that really count. They have no idea if they are compatible on very important matters because their focus is on touching rather than talking.

For a long time, guys have been trying to get girls to sleep with them by telling them, "We have to find out if we are sexually compatible."

A guy who uses that line needs to enroll in Biology 101. If you have a male and female, guess what—they're sexually compatible. Women, when a guy uses that line, what he is really saying is that he wants to use you to meet his sexual desires. Please allow me to be very, very blunt. He simply wants to have an orgasm with you. Don't fall for that nonsense. Sexually, any man and woman are physically compatible.

And one more thing.

Get to know their heart. Do you really know their heart? Do you know what's down deep inside of them? Is Christ ruling and reigning on the throne of their heart? Do you know their hopes and dreams? Have they shared their failures of the past and fears of the future?

If they make a commitment, will they keep a commitment? If they don't demonstrate that in their life, then run. If you're not sure, you don't know enough about them yet. Back off on the physical and get to know their heart. Find out if their heart is compatible with your heart.

Your whole life is on the line here. And so is the life of your future children. This is nothing to play around with—but if you seek the Lord with your whole heart and listen to wise counsel, He will instruct you.

He will make known to you the path of life (Psalm 16:11).

So there are some ground rules. And if you follow them it will guarantee that you will be happily married at forty.

Not quite.

Those ground rules are of strategic importance. But they are simply the foundational principles you build on as you look for a potential mate.

They are commonsense principles. And they can save your life.

Psalm 127:1 sums it all up:

Unless the Lord builds the house,
They labor in vain who build it.

If you want to ruin
your life by forty,
ignore God's directives
about marriage.

CHAPTER 7

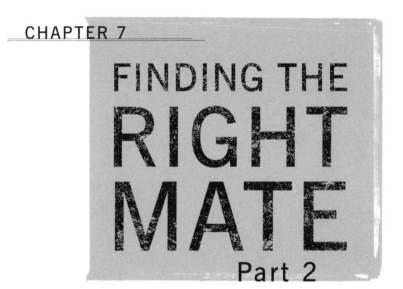

FINDING THE RIGHT MATE
Part 2

Jonathan Edwards had a marriage made in heaven.

John Wesley had a marriage that was living hell.

Both men were born in 1703.

Both men knew the Scriptures.

But when it came to choosing a mate Edwards used wisdom.

John Wesley didn't. And he paid the price for such a foolish move.

Edwards was greatly used by God here in the States, and his writings were influential in many nations, as they are to this day. He was probably the greatest philosopher and theologian that America ever produced. He loved to write and study and pastor his church. He traveled some but always wanted to be home with his wife, Sarah. On most days in the late afternoon, they would take an hour and go horseback riding to simply enjoy one another's company.

John Wesley also liked to ride horses. He traveled England by horseback for fifty-three years, often preaching four to five times a day. It was estimated that he rode close to a quarter of a million miles. But he often rode to get away from home. If you had a wife that was seen dragging you by the hair perhaps you would get on a horse and ride a quarter of a million miles too.[22]

Jonathan and Sarah Edwards were friends and lovers. They had eleven children.

John and Molly Wesley were enemies, and one wonders if they were ever lovers. They had no children. There's a reason for that. If you never have sex, you probably won't have children. (I think that's known as cause and effect.) Some couples enjoy a wonderful sexual relationship but are never able to have children. One gets the strong impression that was not the reason John and Molly did not have children.

Four months after marrying Molly, John wrote a letter to his brother, Charles. In it, he made this statement: "Love is rot."[23]

That's not the kind of comment that leads to conversation, romance, and intimacy.

On one occasion when John was in Bristol, he received an urgent message that Molly was near death due to an extraordinarily high fever. He immediately got on his horse and rode back home. By the time he arrived the fever had broken. An hour later he was on his horse headed back to Bristol. No wonder she was resentful.

THE BIG QUESTION

The big question still remains for you: *How will I know when I meet the right person?*

You need to know something right up front.

God will lead you. But He wants you to use wisdom.

Jonathan and Sarah followed wisdom from the start of their relationship. When he was twenty-three and Sarah was seventeen, they were married. They had courted and spent many hours together for nearly four years. In spending time together, they got to know the other's heart. They knew each other like a book. When they first met, Sarah was just thirteen. Although she was young, they took time to let their relationship mature. One gets the sense that they were both seeking the Lord and His wisdom.

So what happened to John Wesley? John Wesley was a great man and a godly man. But when it came to women he bordered on stupid. Instead of seeking wisdom and wise counsel, he consistently made poor choices in relationships. He was always aboveboard in his morality and purity, but he seemed to presume upon the Lord's wisdom by making blunder after blunder. He ran at the last minute from serious romances when he was twenty-five, thirty-five, and forty-five.[24] At forty-seven, on a whim and in absolute secret, he married Molly.

In each of the three prior relationships, he was convinced that each of the young women would make an excellent wife. In at least two of the relationships, he would drop hints that he was going to propose marriage, but never followed through. In each situation, after years of waiting as he procrastinated and refused to commit, each woman married another young man, once due to the encouragement of John's brother. According to his journals, John knew that he should move ahead. But he went against all wisdom and refused to do so. And in each case, he lost the woman he loved.[25] God wanted John Wesley to walk in wisdom, and he normally did—except when it came to choosing a marriage partner.

At the age of forty-seven, he married Molly very quickly without getting any counsel. He didn't marry her because God made him do so against his will. He married her because he was impulsive and unwise. It's very apparent that he didn't seek the Lord's counsel. And as a result, he was chained to a miserable woman for the rest of his life.

If you ignore His wisdom and leading, you will be stuck with the consequences of your decision to not seek His best.

But it didn't have to be that way for John.

He would have been better off if he had stayed single. But he went against wisdom and married a hard and difficult woman. And his misery was of his own making. He had no one to blame except himself. Quite frankly, he didn't use his head or his heart.

LIFE WITHOUT MARRIAGE

Some people ask me, "But what if God doesn't intend for me to marry?"

My answer is the answer of Jesus. "Do not be worried about your life…but seek first His kingdom and His righteousness, and all these things will be added to you" (Matthew 6:25, 33).

Does God have a plan for you that is rich with purpose and meaning? Absolutely. Then let your focus be right there. Focus on God and His goodness and wisdom. If He wants you married, He has been working from before the creation of the world to make that happen. If you are the exception and marriage is not in His plan for you, then don't you think He will take care of you and give you a full life of unforeseen and rich meaning not yet imagined? Do you not know that "He is able to do exceeding abundantly beyond all that we ask or think" (Ephesians 3:20)?

He's able to do all of that and even more.

It's better to be single and content than married and miserable.

Marriage will not fulfill you. *God* will. Marriage cannot meet your deepest needs. Only *God* can do that.

If you look to your partner to fulfill these things, you are going to be disappointed every time.

People don't just meet and fall in love and fit perfectly together and have great sex and get along beautifully together. Nothing could be more obvious, but it's a reality we choose to ignore. Align yourself to that fact. Great marriages don't just happen. We are sinful beings, and we fight an Enemy who wants to divide and destroy our marriages. That's why if you want to have a great marriage, you're going to have to take up your cross and follow after Christ. Great marriage, to borrow Eugene Peterson's phrase, requires a long obedience in the right direction. There are no shortcuts.

You want to have a great marriage? Then don't focus on pursuing a partner. Focus on pursuing God. Let Him take care of bringing the right person into your life, in the right place, at the right time.

Do you play a role in finding the right mate? Yes, you do.

Your role is to think wisely and live well.

Jonathan and Sarah Edward did that.

John and Molly Wesley didn't—at least not when it came to choosing a mate.

Thinking wisely involves *starting with the right question*.

Living well involves *being the right person*.

BEGIN WITH THE RIGHT QUESTION

When you are considering marrying someone for life, you want to be thinking clearly and carefully. Clarity is the goal.

The great Scottish reformer, John Knox, once referred to foolish men with these sharp words:

"A certain type of man is always able to trim his sails to suit the prevailing winds, and he takes pride in the fact that he is adept at it. He does not know where he is going, but he is making good time."[26]

If you don't know where you are going, there is no reason in the world to try and hurry to get there.

So where are you going on the question of marriage? Well, to get some clarity and clear thinking, you have to ask the right questions. The first question is not, *Who am I going to marry?*

The first question is, *What kind of marriage do I want to have?*

That question will lead you down a path of wisdom to the next right questions—and those questions will lead you to your partner for life.

When Jonathan Edwards was on his deathbed, he looked back over his thirty-one years of marriage to Sarah and described it as "an uncommon union."

What kind of marriage *do* you want to have? In twenty years, what do you want your marriage to look like? Whenever I ask this question, certain answers quickly rise to the surface, and they are consistently the same. In twenty years:

- I want my mate to be my best friend.
- I want to still be able to laugh and enjoy life together.
- I want a marriage of absolute trust because I know my partner is committed to me alone.
- I want to feel affirmed instead of attacked, understood rather than misunderstood, loved instead of taken for granted, valued rather than demeaned, respected instead of depreciated. I want our home to be a place of refuge, not a place of chaos.
- I want a marriage characterized by resolved conflict, not a constant fighting or hiding behind hurts and misunderstandings.
- I want us to be a team, not two people going in different directions.
- I want a marriage characterized by honesty and transparency, where sin can be exposed and forgiven, and wounds can be healed.
- I want a marriage that encourages me to be a better person and inspires me to use my gifts to their fullest potential.
- If you are a man, you want a wife who has chosen to make you

and your children the top priority of her life. You want a woman who will honor you and encourage your leadership. You want her to understand and value your masculinity. You want her to be tender and teachable.

♦ If you are a woman, you want a husband who has chosen to make you and your children the top priority in his life. You want him to value you, listen to you, love you, lead you, protect you, and embrace your femininity. You want him to be tender and teachable.

♦ You want your kids to look at your marriage and say, "That's the kind of marriage I want to have someday."

This kind of marriage is an uncommon union. It takes time to build an uncommon union between a husband and wife. It doesn't happen overnight. It only happens if you're in it for the long haul.

That leads you to the *next* questions: (1) What kind of person do I need to *look for* to have this kind of marriage? And, (2) What kind of person do I need *to be*? Let me give you a few examples.

Do you want to have a marriage characterized by trust? Then if you are a young woman, ask yourself a few questions. Do I flirt around? Do I give mixed messages? Likewise, is this guy a man of his word? Is he constant in his affections, or does he have wandering eyes? Does he respect sexual boundaries?

Trust is something that has to be earned. But once earned, it is the wall of safety that surrounds and protects a good marriage. Satan can throw darts all day long, but they will simply bounce off the impregnable wall of trust. Guys, when you tell a woman you love her, are you a one-woman kind of man with your eyes and your mind? Are you a player, or are you a man of your word?

What about honesty and transparency? Are you dating someone who is able to be transparent and real? Are you willing to expose your own true inner self? If that's hard for you—and it is for most of us—now is the time to start being who you really are. If he rejects that, he's not the man for you. If she can't accept who you really are, then she will make you miserable. Don't wait five or ten or fifteen years to learn how to be transparent. Take the risk. God will honor you for it. He will use it to lead you to the right partner for life.

Do you want a marriage where the two of you aren't constantly fighting? Then how do you handle an argument right now? Do you hide behind hurt and avoid the conflict altogether? Do you get defensive or controlling? If the primary way you handle conflict in this relationship is by avoiding the hard issues and falling back on physical intimacy, you're in for hard times. Believe me, that's not going to work when you get married.

And here's why. It goes right back to cause and effect.

Inside Out

Let's put this down where the rubber meets the road. If you are dating or considering marrying someone right now, what is he or she like at the very core? You need to discern if the *outside* matches what's on the *inside.* We said in the last chapter that you should be dating only Christians. But being a Christian doesn't guarantee a happy marriage.

Open your eyes and look at the clear signs.

If wisdom is giving you a red light, don't drive through the intersection.

Girls, is this guy going to value you and treat you with respect? Look at how he treats his mom. That's a pretty good clue. Actually it's more than a clue. It's almost prophetic. The way that a guy treats his mother is the way that he will treat you. Does he not respect her? Then he will not respect you. Does he belittle her input and opinions? Then he will do the same with you. But on the other hand, if he loves his mother and honors her and respects her—then that's what you can expect from him toward you.

You guys should look at how a young woman relates to her father. Is she close to him? Does she feel loved by him? Or has she been terribly hurt by him? If she has, that simply means that she will bring the hurt into the marriage. If her father was unloving and abusive, you are going to have clean up his mess. She may, at times, have trouble trusting you because she doesn't trust her father. But as you are trustworthy, she will see that you are different from her father.

Everybody has stuff that they bring into a marriage. It's good to find out as much as you can about the stuff before you get married. Then you are walking into marriage with your eyes open. That just makes sense, doesn't it?

WHAT ARE THE NON-NEGOTIABLES?

Not long ago, a young woman asked me, "If there is one thing I should look for in a man, what would it be?" I didn't even bat an eyelid. "That's easy," I said. "Look for teachability." A guy who is teachable will grow. A teachable guy has a heart for God and a desire to conquer sin in his life. A teachable man is secure enough to appreciate your input and value your insight. If teachability isn't there, you are headed for a hellish marriage, and misery will be your company all your days.

> In a man, look for TEACHABILITY. In a woman, look for **secure femininity.**

When a guy asks me that same question, my immediate answer is, "Look for secure femininity." You don't want a woman who needs to be in control and call the shots. If you marry that kind of woman, prepare for the fight of your life—or a white flag. What you need is a woman who knows who she is and is strong of character, yet feminine to the core. You need a woman who desires for you to be every bit the man God created you to be. Such a woman will be a blessing to you all your days.

I've noticed a troubling trend among some young men these days. There's a tendency among some Christian guys to gravitate toward immature, unthinking, weak women, who require little of them in terms of maturity.

Why do they avoid the mature Christian women around them? For one thing, they are often ashamed of the sin they haven't conquered (most often it is habitual pornography), and they are afraid of a godly woman getting too close. For another thing, the thought of leading such a woman cuts the knees right out from under them. They don't know how to lead. And they are afraid they will fail miserably at it, perhaps like their father did. Leadership is learned, and if you want to follow Christ, He will turn you into a godly leader. But it doesn't happen overnight.

Can I give you guys a tip? Sure, there are some immature Christian women who have unrealistic expectations. But most Christian women aren't looking for a guy who's going to lead them in biblical devotions or discussions of theology. A good woman just wants a man who realizes his calling to servant leadership, and is willing to pursue God with all his heart. She's looking for a guy who is real, not a phony. She knows you are human and struggling with sin. So is she. What matters most to her is that at an appropriate point, you are willing to be vulnerable about your sin, that you deplore it and want to wrestle it to the ground. A good woman places the highest value on a man who is teachable and tender to the Spirit of God. You have no idea how much respect that woman has for such a guy. Genuineness and humility always trump a cool cover.

Let me sum it up in one sentence: *A good woman longs for a man who is willing to accept the challenge of becoming a man of God, with her by his side.*

Guys, if you were to get up the nerve to get close to a truly good woman, you would discover this surprising truth. Don't let a girl's maturity run you off. Welcome it. That is the very kind of woman you need for a life partner.

Find a woman who loves the Lord, loves life, and will love you. And when you find her, pursue her. Don't be passive. Make the call. Take the first step. Nothing's going to happen until you do. This is where John Wesley blew it three times. For some reason, he became passive when he found a great woman. That's not the time to become passive. When you find a woman who loves the Lord and makes your heart beat faster, it's time to be a man and get with the program.

OPPOSITES DISTRACT

There is a myth that needs to be put in the Dumpster. Do opposites attract? They may or may not. But a man and a woman who are seriously opposite will not naturally have the stuff for a great marriage. That is a myth. Opposites may attract, but they can also seriously distract.

Being like-minded in passions, personality, and calling *do* matter. Look long and hard at these things before you step onto the road of life with someone.

Being opposite is not necessarily good. Opposite sex *is* good: "God created them male and female," and He called this "good." But opposite minds and calling are an omen for unforeseen hardship and heartache up ahead.

I will never forget sitting with my future wife in the office of Dr. Grant Howard, our outstanding professor in marriage and family and our premarital counselor. Dr. Howard had just given us the results of a personality test we had each taken separately. The tests showed us to be similar in every category but one, and we were worried.

"Is this a bad sign?" we asked. "Does this mean we won't complement one another, or challenge each other to grow?"

"Are you kidding? Absolutely not!" he said. "Trust me. Be thankful that you have so much in common. The more alike you are, the better you will be able to understand each other and work together as a team. Listen to me when I tell you that we are different enough as male and female, with different personalities, backgrounds, and baggage we carry into marriage. I've observed over the years that the more alike two people are, the happier their marriage will be. Don't worry about challenge. There will be plenty of that as it is."

He was exactly right.

Being opposite in your thinking and calling creates a battle scene the likes of which you may not fathom right now. Think about the fact that in marriage you will be making huge decisions together: where you live, where you worship, how you parent, who will raise your children, how you spend your money, how you get through deep personal disappointments and hardships in life. If you add to the mix two people who don't share the same worldview, the same values, the same callings and leanings, the same perspective on male and female roles, a deep understanding of each other—you have a troubled marriage in the making.

WISE THINKING

Let me encourage you to think wisely about a mate. Don't make John Wesley's mistake.

Look for a partner who shares your heart, your worldview, your loves and passions in life, your leanings and interests. Be careful of being drawn to someone primarily out of a neediness for something you lack and they possess. Let me give you several examples that I've seen time and time again over the years.

A controlling person marries someone who is easily controlled. A shy person who loves books and learning latches onto the coattails of a socially skilled person who hates books and learning. A person with a particular calling in life marries someone who is appealing, but not of the same mind or suited for that calling.

Abraham Lincoln married someone very different than himself. He once said, "Marriage is neither heaven nor hell; it is simply purgatory."

If you marry someone who is your opposite, believe me, the

attraction will soon lead to a *distraction* of huge proportions, and grief untold. Can you work through these things once you are married? You must. You are committed for life.

The bottom line is this: Look for someone with whom you are *like-minded*. Someone who is your soul mate—someone who understands what makes you tick. If your dating relationship is already characterized by ongoing conflict and continual misunderstandings, that's a huge red flag. Don't ignore it.

Does this mean you shouldn't look for someone who completes or complements you? Of course not. But be wise. Decide what the non-negotiables are for you as a unique individual—both in personality and calling in this life. And be on guard if you are attracted to someone who is so extremely opposite to you that you will end up having to fight every day of your life just to understand each another.

STATE OF YOUR UNION

So what does your dating relationship look like right now?

Is it characterized by honesty, acceptance, and safety, a commitment to resolving conflict, a sense of mission *together* as a couple, a desire to embrace biblical manhood and womanhood? Are you able to talk about your past and begin a process of healing with this person by your side? Are you challenged to grow closer to Christ? Does he or she make you a better person? Do you have a similar worldview and vision for where you are going in life?

Then you are on a great track.

When you get right down to it, *what you are before you are married is what you will be after you are married.*

Don't marry your dream of what they could become.

You don't marry a dream. You marry a person.

Right now is as good as it gets.

Let's be honest. You're looking pretty good right now. You're on your best behavior. So are they. You're trying to impress each other. If the non-negotiables aren't there now, don't presume upon God to cause the things you need to miraculously appear down the road of life.

What you see—when you really look with both eyes open—is what you get. So look very closely and proceed wisely.

How do you find the right mate? You pursue God, ask the right questions, keep your eyes wide open, and trust in His providential goodness.

Ask Him to give you an "uncommon union."

That's what Jonathan and Sarah Edwards had for thirty-one years. Mary and I are coming up on thirty years of marriage.

When we got married, we wanted to have an uncommon union like Jonathan and Sarah.

So they sort of became our role models.

Every afternoon they rode horses together.

Most afternoons we ride horses together. My pickup has close to three hundred horses under the hood.

Jonathan and Sarah had eleven children, so we had eleven children (actually we had three, but most of the time it seemed like eleven).

I do a fair amount of traveling, but I get home to Mary as soon as I can.

That's what it's like when you have an uncommon union.

If you want to ruin
your life by forty,
develop a mind-set that
isn't teachable.

> *"It is morally impossible to exercise trust in God while there is failure to wait upon Him for guidance and direction."*
>
> D. E. HOSTE

CHAPTER 8

FOLLOW THE LEADER

Fred Olford was a twenty-two-year-old Englishman preparing to enter the business world. He was staying for a time at his cousin's country estate in England. He was enjoying the calm of the rolling hills and wheat fields that were ripe for harvest. But one night a violent thunder and hailstorm rolled in. The next morning he opened the bedroom curtain to see that the brown waves of wheat had been completely destroyed by hail.

At that moment he was struck that God wanted him to go to Africa to reap the harvest for Christ.

Now that may seem like a strange way to figure out what God wants you to do. But a process had been going on for months in Fred's heart. He had developed a desire, almost a pull, to go to Africa and make known the gospel to those who had never heard it. With all of that desire, thought, and prayer behind him, at that moment he immediately knew that was his life work. Everything he had been processing just suddenly "clicked." He was going to Africa. It was something he felt called to do and something he wanted to do.

He immediately began preparing, and within two years he found himself in central Africa. But not just Africa—he was in remote Africa. No strolls in the parks of London and no leisurely afternoons in the English countryside. He was going to the middle of nowhere.

Fred was like any normal twenty-four-year-old man. He had a desire to find a wife and start a family. As great as that desire was, his desire to follow Christ where He led was even greater.

Across the Atlantic Ocean in a typical American home, a young girl was growing up. Bessie Santmire was just seven when her mother tragically died. She went to live with her older sister. Two years later, her sister led her to Jesus Christ. At the age of sixteen, Bessie had a very strong desire to serve the Lord in Africa. Not everyone understood her thinking. It was so unusual for a young, unmarried American girl to think of going to the other side of the world.

But Bessie knew it was a calling from the Lord and the deep desire of her heart. Yes, she had a desire to one day be a wife and a mother. But at the same time, she had this inner drive to prepare for life in Africa. She began to pursue the education that would prepare her for work in another land. Several years later, her training was cut short when a missionary couple invited her to join them as they returned to Africa.

It was a difficult journey to Angola. But the journey became even more difficult as they made their way into the interior. It took them a week of traveling twenty-five miles a day to reach the base missionary station. And they walked every step. But Bessie still had a ways to go when they arrived at the remote station. She and the other missionaries were assigned to go even deeper into the interior, into the wild country to a rough little village called Luma-Cassai.

When she walked into the remote, primitive village, thousands of miles away from America and her friends and any prospects of marriage—there stood Fred Olford.

He looked at her and she looked at him. Two years later they were married. They stayed happily married for thirty-five years until Fred went home to be with the Lord.[27]

The point of that story is not that God is calling you to Africa. The point is that if you will follow Him no matter where He leads you, you will discover that the plan He has for you is greater than anything you could ever come up with on your own. Fred was in England and Bessie was in America. They were an ocean apart and knew nothing of each other when they both yielded their lives completely to the Lord. Both were in their early twenties. And they both had a decision to make.

Would they do what He said?

Would they go where He led?

Nearly a century ago, Fred and Bessie were facing the big questions of their twenties—what would they do and who would they marry. They couldn't see the future just as you can't see the future. But they decided to follow their Shepherd—fully and completely. Ultimately, that's the really big issue. It's even bigger than what you will do or who you will marry.

But if you will yield your life to Christ and put Him first in your life, the other issues will take care of themselves. He may not lead you to go halfway around the world. But He will lead you.

How, then, does the invisible God speak to us today? *How* does He lead?

WALKING THROUGH UNCHARTED TERRITORY

There are several general principles that are clear throughout the Scriptures.

1. *He guides us through His written Word.*

Now if you want to get confused about guidance, just turn on the television and listen to a Christian talk show. I heard a very popular preacher recently say, "Then God spoke to me, and He told me to go buy that plane. And I said, 'But God, I already have a plane.' And He said, "Yes, but I want you to have another one.'" The "name it and claim it" crowd are constantly claiming that God speaks audibly to them. But where in the Bible are we told to seek riches? Where does it say that wealth is an indication of spirituality and faith? Jesus said, "Do not store up for yourselves treasures on earth. . . . But store up for yourselves treasures in heaven. . . . No one can serve two masters. Either he will hate the one and love the other, or he will be devoted to the one and despise the other. You cannot serve both God and Money."

God has never spoken to me audibly. Never. Not once. But He has spoken to me hundreds of times through His inspired written Word. When He speaks in His Word, it's very clear. I don't have to wonder whose voice I am hearing.

Here's what I mean. His Word leads me into wise choices, habits, and patterns of life. It warns me of pitfalls. It instructs me about good decisions and bad decisions. It tells me what kind of people to avoid and what kind to hang out with. It helps me in the middle of trials.

> *"Thy testimonies are my delight;*
> *They are my counselors . . .*
> *I have more insight than all my teachers,*
> *For Thy testimonies are my meditation." (Psalm 119:24, 99)*

When you long to know the mind of God regarding a decision in your life, stay close to His Word.

2. *He guides us through our own pliable, teachable spirit.*

> *"I will instruct you and teach you in the way which you should go;*
> *I will counsel you with my eye upon you." (Psalm 32:8)*

God promises to instruct us. But there is one stipulation.

The condition is not on God—it's on us. The Lord lays it out to David in the very next verse: "Do not be as a horse or as the mule which have no understanding, whose trappings include bit and bridle to hold them in check, otherwise they will not come near you."

God puts the cards on the table. *Yes,* He says, *I'll be your guide. But once I show you the way, don't be like a horse that fights his rider.*

I remember when I was in high school going with a bunch of friends over to the beach to rent some horses. I had ridden maybe twice in my life. Let me tell you about the horses they used to rent over at Half Moon Bay, California. Those horses had absolutely no interest in going where the riders wanted them to go. Those horses had a mind of their own. There were maybe ten of us in the group, and our plan was to ride leisurely together along the beach. Within five minutes we were all scattered over at least a half of mile. I was leading my horse to go right toward where the waves were breaking. But my horse wanted to go left because about three hundreds yards away was his favorite hill that was brimming over with clover. For the next hour all I did was fight that horse. I wanted to go right—he wanted to go left.

To be more specific, I was fighting the horse's heart.

Now that is exactly what God was telling David. Do you want guidance? In essence the Lord is saying, I'll be your guide. If you listen to me you can have a significant life and avoid a lot of unnecessary pain. But when I show you, don't be like the horse that wants to go left when I'm telling you to go right. You see that it comes back to the heart, doesn't it?

There's no reason to ask the Lord for guidance if you aren't willing to obey Him. And the evidence that your heart isn't in it is that you are stubborn in your heart and resistant in your response to His guidance. Obey Him in the little things. Obey Him in the daily stuff. Be faithful, and He will be faithful to honor you and lead you.

3. *He guides us through wise counselors.*

In the body of Christ, older men are to teach younger men. And older women are to teach younger women. That's because the older ones have made a lot of mistakes and experienced far more of life. They have the wisdom that can only come from hindsight and maturity. Don't simply strike out on your own and ignore the advice of the mature people in your life who love you. God uses mentors. Do you have a mentor? Someone in your life who understands you well? Seek out wise counselors when you have a big decision in front of you. And take their advice to heart.

One more word on this, and it could be the subject of an entire book. The friends you choose are critical. Wrong friends take you down the wrong path, and right friends will walk with you on the right path.

First Corinthians 15:33 says it best: "Do not be deceived: 'Bad company corrupts good morals.'" David and Jonathan were best friends. They looked out for each other. David got involved with Bathsheba after Jonathan was killed in battle. I wonder what would have happened to David if Jonathan had been around to steer him away from temptation? The right friends can make all the difference in the world.

4. *He often guides us through the timing of circumstances, including delays and disappointments.*

Sometimes God's greatest blessings come out of a deep disappointment. You see it in the life of Joseph and Moses. God's delays are not God's denials. Wait on Him for His timing. His timing is worth waiting for because it is perfect.

5. *He leads us through our requests.*

Ask Him in specific ways to open doors and opportunities for you.

> *Ask . . . seek . . . knock. What man is there among you who, when his son asks for a loaf, will give him a stone? . . . If you then, being evil, know how to give good gifts to your children, how much more will your Father who is in heaven give what is good to those who ask Him! (Matthew 7:7–11)*

You can trust Him to answer in the right way and at the right time. As Jan Karon says, "Pray that prayer that God always answers—'not my will, but Thine be done.'"

6. *He guides us through our gifts, propensities, and personalities.*

This is what we covered back in chapter 5.

7. *He guides us through the encouragement of others.*

When other people notice our gifts and point them out often to us, God is using them to light a fire under us. When other people recognize your gifts, don't ignore that. Especially if it comes from two or three people within a few days or weeks.

8. *He even uses our weaknesses, and our willingness to see what we aren't good at as a means to guide us.*

When all is said and done, God uses the instincts of your heart—if you are walking with Him. "Love God and do what you want," said Saint Augustine.

One thing you can be sure of. He will never guide you into sin. Never.

So how do you navigate on a journey that is nothing less than life and death? How do you make wise decisions under pressure and temptation? How do you know to take the left fork or the right fork when they both look the same?

The great pastor of three centuries ago, John Flavel, gave this advice to those seeking to know God's direction in their lives. Now this can read a little rough because it is three centuries old. But I assure you that it is well worth the effort of reading it carefully.

> There is nothing **greater** in life than to see the PROVIDENCE of God at work when you've asked for guidance.

"The way we now have to know the will of God concerning us in difficult cases, is to search and study the Scriptures, and where we find no particular rule to guide us in this or that particular case, there we are to apply general rules."[28] And what are those rules? Flavel lays out five that contain good sense and wisdom. If you follow these closely with your whole heart, you can be confident that you will not ruin your life by foolish decisions:

If therefore, in doubtful cases, you would discover God's will, govern yourselves in your search after it by these rules:

1. *Get the true fear of God upon your hearts; be really afraid of offending Him.*

2. *Study the Word more, and the concerns and interests of the world less.*

3. *Reduce what you know into practice, and you shall know what is your duty to practice.*

4. *Pray for illumination and direction in the way that you should go.*

5. *And this being done, follow providence as far as it agrees with the Word, and no further.* [29]

It was the providence of God that brought Fred and Bessie together in the middle of an obscure village of huts in remote Africa.

You serve the same God. He promises to lead you. He probably won't take you to Africa. But if He did, would you be willing to go?

There is nothing greater in life than to see the providence of God at work when you've asked for guidance.

So when all else fails, read the directions.

And follow the Leader.

If you want to ruin
your life by forty,
hide your heart
instead of guarding it.

"The greatest struggle the most."
JOHN PIPER

CHAPTER 9

HONEST STRUGGLES

Do you recall the stories I shared early on in the book about those individuals who started strong but didn't finish strong? Do you remember the statement that for every ten who start strong in their twenties, only one out of ten will finish strong? Chuck Templeton and Bron Clifford were enormously gifted, but they shipwrecked before they were forty.

So what went wrong and how do you keep it from happening to you?

Here's the answer and it comes from Proverbs 4:23:

Watch over your heart with all diligence
For from it flow the springs of life.

Pure and simple, the reason that these individuals went down before the age of forty is that they didn't guard their hearts.

THE STRUGGLES OF LIFE

Don't kid yourself.

Everybody struggles.

Everybody has issues.

And I mean everybody.

It never ceases to amaze me what lies beneath the surface of people I meet.

- A warm, personable young man happens to sit next to me at a banquet table. No one at that table would have guessed that he had just lost his wife and four children in a flash flood only a few months before.
- A beautiful young woman with a passion for the Lord is deeply involved in ministering to young girls. Who would imagine that she was raped as a young girl and still struggles deeply with those scars?
- A socially engaging and fearless young man seems to connect so easily with people and understand what makes them tick. Yet underneath the surface is a struggle with social anxiety that few would ever suspect.
- A gifted female athlete who gave her life to Christ in college now leads a ministry to college girls. It would surprise anyone who meets this lean, attractive young woman to know that she has deeply struggled for years with issues of body image.
- A spiritually mature young father has a ministry to hurting

people. If he did not openly tell his story, no one would imagine that he once struggled with homosexuality. Sexually abused by another man when he was a boy, he spent the next decade and a half of his life in a tortured homosexual lifestyle until he found deliverance through Jesus Christ. He tells his story so that people will know that Christ can deliver a man out of the most hopeless places of sin and despair.

Everyone has a story. Each of us is like an iceberg, with eight-ninths of our true selves hidden beneath the surface waters. In public we may appear to others as if we haven't a care in the world. But underneath the exterior of every person is a story of struggle and pain. We are all broken people, living in a broken world.

Most people think I am this confident, invulnerable guy who travels and speaks because he has it all together. Because I write books and am privileged to speak all over the nation they get this strange idea that I never struggle. Well, I do struggle. I wish that I didn't, but I do.

They are surprised to learn that early in our marriage I went through a two-year period of depression and fell into the "pit of despair," as the psalmist David would say. During those years I couldn't get a church pastorate job to save my life, and I became convinced that my call to ministry was over. I had no idea that God was getting me ready for a work, not setting me aside permanently. Depression engulfed me to such a degree that I couldn't study Scripture, and on some days I would cry for several hours. God brought me through that difficult, humbling chapter, and accrued to my life the fruit of empathy for others and a sense of complete dependence upon Him I had not possessed before. I realize now that God was doing deep surgery to prepare me for the work He had for me to do. But I won't kid you. It was a painful time I would not ever wish to relive.

Do I struggle now? You bet I do. Life continually throws curve balls and unexpected difficulties my way. And not a day goes by that I don't struggle with my own personal weaknesses and sin. I can't organize my way out of a paper bag; my temper has a very short leash; I regularly fight the urge to worry about finances and a hundred other things; and I'm vulnerable to sexual temptation—just like every other guy on planet Earth. That's the short list. You get the picture.

Does that make you uncomfortable? I hope not, because *every* man and woman struggles. And if they say they don't, they're lying. Even Jesus struggled deeply, though He never sinned (Hebrews 2:18).

You, too, have a story. Underneath the seemingly calm and together surface of your life lie the deep struggles of your heart. You may anesthetize yourself or avoid them through constant activity, but when you are alone in your bed in the dark of night and listen to yourself think, they are still there. Some people struggle with doubt about God; some are racked with guilt over habitual hidden sin; some are wounded deeply and struggle with anger or great loss; some live in a perpetual state of anxiety or self-recrimination. All of us struggle. It's a given in life.

Struggles can hit you through your personality and wiring. They can blindside you through reminders of past experiences. They can nail you through a habitual sin, begun when you walked through an open gate long ago.

AN HONEST PLACE

So where can you share the struggle, and where can you be real? Now you'd never walk into a gathering of believers and spill your guts about these things. If the pastor doesn't let on that he struggles (and it is a rare pastor who does), how can the people who sit under him feel free to reveal their struggles? Isn't the goal not to struggle? If it is, then who wants to let on that they haven't quite got it all together? In church, we simply don't tend to do *real*. Not even among Christian friends. And if we can't be real among believers, how in the world can we be real among unbelievers, where winning and success and being cool are everything? No one likes a loser. Everyone loves a winner. There doesn't seem to be any safe place to allow our true selves to be exposed and known, except perhaps inside the office of a biblical counselor, which by the way is a good place to go when things get really bad.

This is a very sad predicament.

It's especially sad because as long as struggles remain hidden in our hearts, we cannot become healthy and free to fulfill the work God has created us to do. Sadder still is the fact that the longer we live alone with our true selves hidden, the bigger and more impenetrable the walls we construct around ourselves become. Saddest of all is the inevitable result at some point down the road when those issues emerge and wreck havoc in our lives and the lives of those around us.

> As long as STRUGGLES remain hidden in our **hearts**, we cannot become healthy and free to fulfill the work GOD has created us to do.

That's what happens to those who crash around forty.

They are hiding their hearts instead of guarding their hearts.

The most important struggle of your life will be to guard your heart. It will take work and it will take honesty.

It is the struggle that you can't ignore. It is the struggle that you can't run away from.

It is the struggle to guard your heart that will determine what happens to you by the time you are forty.

The ones who went down in flames chose to *hide* their hearts rather than *guard* them.

THE HEART OF THE ISSUE

So what is your heart?

The heart is "the seat of reason and the will. The heart is the source, or spring, of motives; the seat of passions; the center of the thought processes; the spring of the conscience."[30]

In other words, the heart is you. It's your personality, your will, your emotions, your mind, and your conscience. Your heart is that unseen engine beneath the hood that takes you down the road of life. It's that seat of your soul that is influenced by affections and wounds, tendencies and habits, the unique wiring of your personality, and your family upbringing. It is that inner sanctuary where every decision is pondered and made. *And it is profoundly affected by what flows into it and is allowed to take root there.*

The book of Proverbs does a thorough job of explaining the battle of the heart. "The heart is the seat of wisdom (2:10); of trust or confidence (3:5); diligence (4:23); perverseness (6:14); wicked imaginations (6:18); lust (6:25); subtlety (7:10); understanding (8:5); deceit (12:20); folly (12:23); heaviness (12:25); bitterness (14:10); sorrow (14:13); backsliding (14:14); cheerfulness (15:13); knowledge (15:14); joy (15:30); pride (16:5); haughtiness (18:12); prudence (18:15); fretfulness (19:3); and envy (23:17)."[31]

All of those things, both good and bad, can come out of our hearts. That's why Solomon tells us to watch over or guard our hearts—it's the wellspring of our lives.

Dr. David Naugle points out that in the Old Testament alone, the word *heart*—when speaking of the centrality of a person's life, and not the physiological organ that pumps blood—appears 855 times. He goes on to say:

According to various New Testament authors, the heart is the psychic center of human affections, the source of the spiritual life, and the seat of the intellect and the will. . . . Jesus . . . was obviously convinced that the cornerstone of a human being, the very foundation of a human life, is to be found in the heart.[32]

WHOLEHEARTEDLY

The battle is to love the Lord our God with *all* of our hearts—not 60 percent or 90 percent. Deuteronomy 6:5 sets out the mark: "You shall love the Lord your God with all your heart and with all your soul and with all your might."

You've heard the phrase, "Put your heart into it!" That means don't just go through the motions. Put everything you have into it—your mind and your will.

The battle is to keep your heart from being divided.

"Seek ye third the kingdom of God," Jesus said.

Actually He didn't say that.

He said, "Seek *first* the kingdom of God and His righteousness" (Matthew 6:33 NKJV).

The battle for your heart is to keep the Lord first and foremost in your life. You are living to please Him. You are living to do His will. As a result, you must guard and protect your heart. That's why you have to battle for your heart.

You have to guard your heart, and when you do, you will guard your mind and your thought life. You will fight to keep a clean conscience before the Lord.

When He convicts you of sin in your heart and your conscience, you deal with the sin right then. You don't ignore it and you don't rationalize it. You guard your heart by fighting sin. It was Martin Luther who said:

> To fight against sin is to fight against the devil, the world, and oneself. The fight against oneself is the worst fight of all.

I am my own worst enemy and you are yours.

When we fight ourselves, as Luther put it, we are battling over our hearts. So what is the heart and how can it play a part in ruining your life by forty?

Charles Bridges was correct when he observed, "The greatest difficulty in conversion is to win the heart to God, and after conversion to keep it with him."[33] That is the very essence of the battle.

No one has said it better than Bridges. In his classic work about Proverbs, he refers to the heart as a citadel, or the headquarters. A citadel is a fortress that often sits on high ground and defends a city. According to Bridges, the heart is the citadel of man:

> Let it be closely garrisoned. Let the sentinel never be sleeping at its post... if the citadel is be taken, the whole town must surrender. If the heart be seized, the whole man—the affections, desires, motives, pursuits—all will be yielded up. The heart is the vital part of the body. A wound here is instant death. Thus—spiritually as well as naturally—out of the heart are the issues of life. It is the great vital spring of the soul, the fountain of actions, the center and the seat of principle, both of sin and holiness (Matthew 12:34–35). The natural heart is a fountain of poison (Matthew 15:19). The purified heart is a well of living water (John 4:14). As is the fountain, so must be the streams. As is the heart, so must be the mouth, the eyes, the feet. Therefore, above all keeping, keep thine heart. Guard the fountain, lest the waters be poisoned.... Many have been the bitter moments from the neglect of this guard. All keeping is vain, *if the heart not be kept.* [34]

Did you catch that? All Bible study, all mission trips, all marriage vows, and all worship is in vain if the heart is not kept.

If the heart is divided before God, will someone keep the marriage vows that they have made? The answer is no. They might say the words, but the words are useless because the heart is divided.

These individuals ruined their lives by forty because they did not fight; they did not struggle to guard their hearts. They gave up fighting sin and just simply gave in. And eventually they were found out.

When someone's private life doesn't match up to his or her public life, it's always a clue that something has gone wrong internally. And it didn't go wrong overnight. It happened over a period of time. In fact, it probably began early and was ignored through the crucial period of the twenties and thirties. Usually by the forties, it can be hidden no longer. It all comes down to the heart.

David was a man after God's own heart. But David did battle over his heart just as you will battle over your heart. He lost the battle when he took Bathsheba into his bed. After a year of covering his sin he was confronted by Nathan the prophet (2 Samuel 11–12). It was then that David broke and confessed his sin before God.

We get a glimpse into the heart of David when he confesses to the Lord in Psalm 51:

> For I know my transgressions, and my sin is ever before me.... Behold, You desire truth in the innermost being, and in the hidden part You will make me know wisdom.... The sacrifices of God are a broken spirit; a broken and contrite heart, O God, You will not despise.

David is confessing that God didn't just want him to proclaim the truth or defend the truth—the Lord wanted him to embrace the truth in his "innermost being." The innermost being is the sincerest reality of who you are. It is the epicenter, the foundation, and the core. Simply put, the innermost being is your heart.

The Bible *never* tires of speaking about it. Proverbs 27:19 says, "As in water face reflects face, so the heart of man reflects man." For this reason, we are told time and again to guard it. It appears again in 1 Samuel 16:7: "For God sees not as man sees, for man looks at the outward appearance, *but the Lord looks at the heart."* In Matthew 15:8, Jesus quoted Isaiah, saying, "This people honors Me with their lips, *but their heart is far away from Me."* Paul recognizes in Romans 8:27 that God searches the hearts of men: "And He who searches the hearts knows what the mind of the Spirit is." The author of Hebrews notes the same idea, saying, "For the word of God is . . . *able to judge the thoughts and intentions of the heart."* The scriptural evidence of God's emphasis upon our hearts is overwhelming. But these verses only skim the surface.

Are you starting to get the impression that your heart is a big deal? What you do with your heart is everything. Now follow this next paragraph carefully.

For this reason, it is not unreasonable to say that the end of all spiritual disciplines, the goal of all biblical imperatives, and thus, the remedy to the vast majority of life's problems is an honest, comprehensive, and courageous confrontation of one's heart.

None of these men or women who started strong when they were in their twenties ever dreamed that their lives would be ruined in their forties. But that's precisely what happened. I remember Joe Aldrich saying one time that Satan would wait forty years to spring a trap. That's what happened to all of these men. They all walked into an ambush. But it was a carefully planned ambush that started with moral shortcuts in their twenties—but the trap wasn't sprung until twenty years later.

For twenty years they failed to confront their hearts. And it turned out to be their downfall.

So you're somewhere around twenty. How do you keep from making the mistakes that these men fell into?

THE GREATEST FEAR

My son Josh wrote this next section, and I think that in it he identifies a core fear for all of us:

It is common knowledge that the greatest fear of men and women today is the fear of death. It usually appears as number one on top ten lists of people's greatest fears. This is understandable. We do not know when our last breath will be or for what reason it

> It may be the BIGGEST fear of all: It is the fear of **dying** to one's self.

will cease, and this hanging ignorance of the end leaves many in a lingering tension. But there is one fear that always fails to make the top ten lists, and yet, it may be the biggest fear of all:

It is the fear of dying to one's self.

No one wants to do it because of the challenge it involves. But dying to one's self is the very thing Christ commanded His followers to do. It is the essential discipline of the Christian life. This is why Jesus said in Luke 9:23–24, "If anyone wishes to come after Me, he must deny himself and take up his cross daily and follow Me. For whoever wishes to save his life will lose it, but whoever loses his life for My sake, he is the one who will save it."

I think that Josh nailed it. This is where the men who ruined their lives by forty went down.

When we are trapped in the clutches of sin, and the sin is becoming more and more habitual, the only way out is to deny yourself. When you are trapped in a certain sin and its power continues to grow in your life, the last thing you would desire would be for someone to find out about it. That is what you are afraid of—someone will find out what you are secretly doing in private. To break free from that sin, you are going to have to deny yourself and your desire of secrecy and make that sin known to someone else. And in order to do that, it is going to take brazen honesty.

But the Enemy lies to you and says that if someone finds out you will be shamed forever. If others find out, you will lose your life and your reputation. That's what he will say to you. He wants you to keep it hidden and private.

The reason these men didn't finish strong is that the majority of them developed private, sinful habits in their twenties that led to their downfall. And they covered up the fact they were struggling. You don't want to make that same mistake.

We all struggle with sin, and we all get off the path. We fall prey to temptation and do things we shouldn't do. We have all ignored the truth and fallen into sin. We all have done things we are ashamed of and deeply regret.

What does the Lord say to us when we are in that horrible trap of sin?

James 5:16 says, "Therefore, confess your sins to one another, and pray for one another so that you may be healed." When we sin, we can't ignore it. We must confess it to the Lord. And when we confess our sin with a broken heart, we find cleansing and forgiveness. First John 1:9 states that "if we confess our sins, He is faithful and righteous to forgive us our sins and to cleanse us from all unrighteousness."

But sometimes when sin is becoming habitual, we can't fight it alone. When habitual sin is killing you, it's time to get some help so you can kill sin.

KILL IT

So how do you put sin to death? It's tough, especially when we have given sin a prominent place, to kill it by ourselves. We need help from others who care for us. That's why James says "confess your sins to one another." Sometimes we are ashamed that we have failed to guard our hearts and we don't want others to find out. So the Enemy holds this over our heads, and this keeps us from confessing the truth to a trusted friend. And therefore we don't get the help or prayer support that we need.

You can't impulsively confess to just anyone. It has to be someone who is seeking to know the Lord and follow Him from their heart. They have to be:

- someone you can trust
- someone who can keep a confidence
- someone who will consistently pray for you and with you
- someone who will walk through life with you

That's the kind of friend who can help you. They will respect your honesty and will realize how difficult a step it was for you to tell them what was going on down deep in your heart. And let me emphasize something one more time. Make sure that they can be trusted to keep their mouths closed and not share your situation with anyone else. If you don't know that for sure about them, find someone else who can be trusted.

Here's the good news. The more honest you can be with yourself before God and His Word, the easier it will be to begin to expose who you really are to someone else. Start with God. The rest will follow. Honesty will begin to spill over into your relationships. Before you know it, a friend will come to you and say, "Thanks for talking about that sin; that was bold of you to admit that. It's kind of leading me to repent as well."

What happens when a friend of yours admits to struggling in a brazenly honest way? Are you repulsed? No. You are first stunned, and then you are relieved. You find yourself respecting that person enormously for having had the humility to be honest. You find yourself being more willing to be real. The result is that one person's honesty opens the floodgates for others to be honest.

Look, if the great apostle Paul can be honest, so can you. Paul admitted to the whole world that he was a murderer, a chief of sinners; he admitted that he struggled with "not practicing what I would like to do," and "doing the very thing I hate" (Romans 7:15). When we read that, we think, *Me too!* Sure, brazen honesty is humbling. But it is also freeing. It moves you out of stubborn pride into teachable humility.

HONESTY IS THE BEST POLICY

I remember when I had to go to a professor and tell him I had not been honest on an exam. Another time I had to confess that I had used a paper that wasn't mine. Those two confessions were exceedingly difficult. I was embarrassed and ashamed. I'm humiliated all over again as I write these words decades later. But the Spirit of God prompted me to acknowledge the truth. I couldn't keep living a lie. I had to kill this sin before it got a grip on me that would ruin my whole life. I put to death the deeds of my flesh in the classroom by going in and confessing what I had done. You kill deception by telling the truth.

It's a great struggle to guard your heart.

It's hard to be honest and face your sin.

It's difficult to die to yourself.

But in the long run, it's worth it.

If you don't believe it, just ask those who ruined their lives by forty.

If you want to ruin
your life by forty,
refuse to take in your
minimum daily
requirement of wisdom.

CHAPTER 10

MINIMUM DAILY REQUIREMENTS

This is the last chapter of this book.

This will also be the shortest chapter of this book.

If I could have you remember just one thing that would help you to keep from ruining your life by forty, here is what it would be.

Read a chapter from the book of Proverbs every day.

Someone has noted that the ultimate book ever written on cause and effect is Proverbs.

The first chapter of this book was all about cause and effect. Every action has a reaction and every choice brings a consequence. When you don't think about cause and effect on a daily basis, you will be sure to ruin your life by forty.

That's why, at the very minimum, you should read a chapter out of Proverbs every day. It will make you think about cause and effect. And it will give you the Word of God, which is the sword of the Spirit, to fight off temptation (Ephesians 6:17).

When Jesus was being tempted by Satan in the wilderness, He quoted from the Old Testament:

> *"Man shall not live by bread alone, but by every word that proceeds from the mouth of God." (Matthew 4:4 NKJV)*

Jesus answered Satan's temptation with Scripture. And the statement that He made was that the Bible is our spiritual food. Every word that proceeds from the mouth of God is in the Bible.

Jesus was saying that the Word of God contains all your amino acids, your vitamins and antioxidants, your A, E, C, chromium, potassium, and selenium—all the nourishment that is needed for your heart. Without it, you weaken and die.

You can't fight off temptation when you are malnourished.

You've heard of the minimum daily requirements that have been suggested by nutritionists. At the very minimum, you need a certain amount of protein, whole grains, fruits, and vegetables to be healthy.

The book of Proverbs is chock-full of God's wisdom.

A chapter a day will give you the wisdom you need for that day.

If you miss a day, don't sweat it.

But don't miss the next day.

A chapter a day in Proverbs is the bare minimum.

You brush your teeth every day.

You take a shower every day.

Read a chapter in Proverbs every day.

If you read it, ponder it, put it into your heart and mind, and then do what it says, you won't ruin your life by forty.

It's that powerful. It's the very wisdom of God.

You can't live without it.

But with it, the possibilities are endless.

NOTES

1. Os Guinness, *The Call: Finding and Fulfilling the Central Purpose of Your Life* (Nashville: Word Publishing, 1998), 194.

2. Steve Farrar, *Finishing Strong* (Sisters, Ore.: Multnomah, 1995).

3. John Haggai, *Lead On!* (Waco, Tex.: Word Books, 1986), 72.

4. R. C. Sproul, *The Invisible Hand* (Dallas: Word Publishing, 1996), 20.

5. Wayne Grudem, *Bible Doctrine: Essential Teachings of the Christian Faith* (Grand Rapids: Zondervan, 1999), 143.

6. John Piper, Justin Taylor, Paul Kjoss Helseth, eds., *Beyond the Bounds: Open Theism and the Undermining of Biblical Christianity* (Wheaton: Crossway, 2003), 380–1.

7. Stephen Mansfield, *Never Give In* (Nashville: Cumberland House, 1995), 54.

8. Ibid.

9. John Piper, "Why I Do Not Say, 'God Did Not Cause the Calamity, But He Can Use It for Good,'" Desiring God Ministries (September 17 2001); http://www.desiringgod.org/library/fresh _words/2001/091701.html

10. Adapted from Steve and Mary Farrar, *Overcoming Overload* (Sisters, Ore.: Multnomah, 2003), 224.

11. Thomas Watson, cited by I. D. E. Thomas, *A Puritan Golden Treasury* (Carlisle, Pa.: Banner of Truth Trust, 1977), 121.

12. Wayne Grudem, *Bible Doctrine: Essential Teachings of the Christian Faith* (Grand Rapids: Zondervan, 1999), 146.

13. John Ryland, cited by J. I. Packer, *God's Plans for You* (Wheaton: Crossway, 2001), 9.

14. Jennifer Woodruff, Thomas Howard, and Edwin Tait, "The Gallery: The Inklings," *Christian History;* http://www.ctlibrary.com/ch/2003/issue78/10.32.html

15. Os Guinness, *The Call: Finding and Fulfilling the Central Purpose of Your Life* (Nashville: Word Publishing, 1998), 5–6.

16. *Business Week*, "Best Leaders" (December 19, 2005), 72.

17. Donald O. Clifton and Paula Nelson, *Soar with Your Strengths* (New York: Delacorte Press, 1992), 3–7.

18. *The Economist* (November 26, 2005), 82.

19. Ibid.

20. Dr. J. Robert Clinton, *The Making of a Leader* (Colorado Springs: Navpress, 1988), 46.

21. Leon Morris, *1 and 2 Thessalonians,* Tyndale New Testament Commentaries (Leicester, England: Inter-Varsity Press, 1984), 81.

22. William J. Petersen, *Martin Luther Had a Wife* (Wheaton: Tyndale, 1983), 42.

23. Ibid.

24. Ibid., 43.

25. *Christian History,* "John Wesley and Women," vol. II, no. 1, 1983, 25.

26. Douglas Wilson, *For Kirk and Covenant: The Stalwart Courage of John Knox* (Nashville: Cumberland House, 2000), 169.

27. John Phillips, *Only One Life: The Biography of Stephen F. Olford* (Neptune, New Jersey: Loizeaux, 1995), 16.

28. John Flavel, *The Mystery of Providence* (Carlisle, Pa.: Banner of Truth Trust, 1963), 186.

29. Ibid., 188.

30. Walter Elwell, *Evangelical Dictionary of Theology* (Grand Rapids: Baker, 1984), 499.
31. Ibid.
32. David K. Naugle, *Worldview: The History of a Concept* (Grand Rapids: Eerdman's, 2002), 268–269.
33. Charles Bridges, *Proverbs* (Carlisle, Pa.: Banner of Truth Trust, 1968), 53.
34. Ibid.